Additional Praise for *Attitudes of Gratitude*

"We have spent the last decades trying to have what we want. This inspiring book shows us how to rejoice in what we have. It's a new millennium manual for living with less grit and more grace. Ryan proves that, no matter how worried we are about the future, feeling and expressing gratitude allows us to celebrate and deeply appreciate the privilege of being in the precious present. Spiritual healers and now modern science teach that a grateful heart leads to loving connection, the ultimate act of well-being. Ryan graciously shows that if we're going to 'have an attitude,' gratitude is the right one."

> —Paul Pearsall, Ph.D., author of *The Pleasure Prescription* and *The Heart's Code*

"*Attitudes of Gratitude* is a most delightful feast of spiritual insights. The quotes at the beginning of each section are outstanding. The personal vignettes are deep yet written simply with the flow of love in each line. It is a book to be savored and not read quickly. This book is pleasing through and through and will help us all to more readily say 'Thank you' every step of our way."

> —Gerald G. Jampolsky, M.D., author of *Love is Letting Go of Fear*

"Thank you for this powerful simple healing. It is a path of joy and clarity."

> —Stephen and Ondrea Levine, authors of *Embracing the Beloved* and *A Year to Live*

"Exquisitely reconnects us to the wonder and satisfaction that can be found in our daily lives."

> —Judy Ford, author of *Wonderful Ways to Be a Family*

"Each section of *Attitudes of Gratitude* acts as a mini-refresher course in the wisdom of focusing on what is really important. I'm thankful to M. J. Ryan because her candid and story-filled book reminds me to return to my heart—the home of gratitude—and, consequently, enhances my connection with all that is wonderful and wise around and within me."

> —Sue Patton Thoele, author of *The Courage to Be Yourself* and *Heart Centered Marriage*

"What M. J. Ryan has done for the world—and it's no small gift—is to forever connect gratitude with joy. She shows us, in brief and engaging reflections, that acknowledging and fostering the feeling of gratitude creates the gift of joy. For the sake of your joy, please don't miss her latest gift, *Attitudes of Gratitude*."

> —David Kundtz, author of *Stopping: How to Be Still When You Have to Keep Going*

"The practice of gratitude is perhaps the most underutilized way to grow spiritually. It is also the fastest way to connect with the joy of being alive. M. J. Ryan provides the inspiration, tools, and heartfelt stories to help anyone make gratitude a wonderful part of their daily life. Honesty and practical wisdom shine throughout the pages of this important book."

> —Jonathan Robinson, author of *Communication Miracles for Couples* and *Shortcuts to Bliss*

"For me, this book could not have come at a better time. I have been working on bringing the ancient practice of gratitude to life in my life and finding that making a list just wasn't enough. Here are hundreds of ways to soften and loosen, to celebrate and pause. Thank you, M. J. Ryan."

—Jennifer Louden, author of *The Woman's Comfort Book* and *The Woman's Retreat Book*

"Thanksgiving is one of the most exciting and powerful antidotes to moral apathy and spiritual indifference available to human beings. The stories in this book testify to this wonderful value that all of us can practice—no matter what our social, economic, cultural, or religious background. Gratitude is ours for the taking, but not to be taken for granted!"

—Elizabeth Espersen, Executive Director, Center for World Thanksgiving

Attitudes of gratitude

How to Give and Receive Joy
Every Day of Your Life

M. J. RYAN

6

Foreword by Sue Bender,
author of *Plain and Simple*

MJF BOOKS
NEW YORK

Fine Communications
322 Eighth Avenue
New York, NY 10001

Attitudes of Gratitude
ISBN-10: 1-56731-372-8
ISBN-13: 978-1-56731-372-7
LC Control Number #99-76027

Cover and interior illustrations: Roger Montoya
Cover art direction: Ame Beanland
Cover and interior design: Suzanne Albertson

This special edition is published by MJF Books in arrangement with Conari Press, an imprint of Red Wheel/Weiser, LLC

Manufactured in the United States of America.

MJF Books is a trademark of Fine Creative Media, Inc.

VB   14   13   12   11   10   9

Life will bring you pain all by itself.
Your responsibility is to create joy.

—Milton Erickson, M.D.

Attitudes of gratitude

3

THE ATTITUDES OF GRATITUDE 49

4

THE PRACTICES OF GRATITUDE 99

5

THE DEEPENING JOURNEY

FOREWORD

DOES IT SOUND STRANGE TO SAY I discovered gratitude from an *exploding turkey*?

My husband Richard and I, both in our sixties and not very practical about financial matters, decided it was finally time to make our will. We went to a lawyer and started the process of creating a living trust for our two sons.

"*What if* the whole family were together at Thanksgiving and the turkey exploded?" the lawyer asked.

"If the four of you were killed at that moment, who would you want to have your worldly goods?" That turned out to be a terrific assignment. A chance to think about the people in our lives, a chance to be grateful and to express our gratitude.

At that time, I was writing my second book, *Everyday Sacred.* I wanted to find what was *sacred* in my everyday life, to look with *fresh eyes* and see what might have been there all along that I had not been able to see. What had I taken for granted? When I began looking, I found teachers everywhere.

A few months later, I learned another lesson in gratitude from a homeless person.

I saw her early every morning at my favorite coffee-house. She looked neat and always sat at the same table reading, but I often wondered if she was a person without a home. One day she walked across the room and asked if I had a pen she could borrow.

"We both like this café," I began. "Why did you choose it?" "I love the light," she said. "It's uplifting." I learned she lived in a shelter and had to leave by 7:00 A.M. She told me she liked this café because she was treated like an individual. "It proves you exist. Sometimes, when I have no money they give me a coffee." And then she added,

"I dream of the day when my life is straightened out and I can walk in here and say, 'This is what I owe you.' Put $500 in the tip jar and say, 'Thank you.'"

M. J. Ryan is a special "gratitude" teacher.

She is the best kind of teacher, one who has struggled to understand gratitude and to live what she is writing. I wrote M. J. Ryan a fan letter after hearing her on a book publishing panel. As I listened to what she said, I was deeply moved. How blessed her authors must be to feel her dedication and high intention. When I learned that she was writing a book and the topic was gratitude, I thought, *Bullseye*.

M. J. Ryan shows us a path to make our practice of gratitude come *alive*.

She brings herself honestly and creatively to the topic, magically transforming gratitude from an abstraction into a useful, palpable reality.

Attitudes of Gratitude shows us specific ways to practice *gratitude* in our everyday lives.

Her wonderful book moves gracefully from the benefits of gratitude and the attitudes that promote it to the daily practices that deepen and nourish our *best* selves.

Every morning, I read one page in each of four small "inspirational" books. The books change, but they always remind me that I am not alone, that there is a spirit larger than myself at work, a universe larger than my immediate self-interest and concerns. I have added *Attitudes of Gratitude* to my morning reading list.

Gratitude makes everyday sacred.

Expressing our gratitude is a gift to the giver.

Gratitude for small things makes every day a gift.

—SUE BENDER, author of
Plain and Simple and
Everyday Sacred

MY THANKS

SINCE 1994, WHEN I WROTE *A Grateful Heart: Daily Blessings for the Evening Meal from Buddha to the Beatles*, I have been thinking and reading about gratitude, and wondering what else I could do to enhance my own sense of thankfulness on a daily level and support it in other people. Many people asked for a sequel to *A Grateful Heart*, but this time I wanted to do something different than a collection of prayers. And so *Attitudes of Gratitude* has been "cooking" in my soul for over four years, until Brenda Knight came along and suggested that I write about gratitude in the way you'll see here. Thank you, BK, for the inspiration and for several stories.

In this work, I have had many teachers, those who have blessed my life with their presence, and those whom I know only from the pages of their books. I thank first of all Dawna Markova for loving friendship and profound thinking on this (and every other) topic, as well as her inspiring embodiment of an asset focus. Her perspectives have become so much my own that it's hard to say where her thinking lets off and mine takes up. She recently spent a day with me, generously offering practices, stories, and perspectives to make this book more useful and less banal. It is a much better book for her contribution.

I also give my loving thanks to Daphne Rose Kingma, for first teaching me the effects of gratitude, for letting me quote from her many books, for imbuing my writing style through example by some of her poetry, and for writing the best thank you notes in the world; to Molly Fumia and Will Glennon, for thinking with me at various spots in the writing of this book; to Sue Patton Thoele, for friendship over the years and allowing me to quote from *The Woman's Book of Spirit*; to my editor Claudia Schaab, who pushed me at the end; and to poet Mark Nepo, for being so generous with his words. Finally, I thank Annette Madden for sharing stories and for being the most vivid example of an "attitude of gratitude" I know.

I also acknowledge Brother David Steindl-Rast, whose insightful writings and tapes on gratefulness, particularly *Gratefulness, the Heart of Prayer*, inform every page of this book; Lewis Smedes' *A Pretty Good Person: What It Takes to Live with Courage, Gratitude, and Integrity*; Adair Lara's *Slowing Down in a Speeded Up World*; David Kundtz's *Stopping: How to Be Still When You Have to Keep Going*; Sarah Ban Brethnach's *Simple Abundance*; Richard Louv's *The Web of Life*; "Positive Image, Positive Action," by David L.

Cooperider; and Joan Borysenko's *Fire in the Soul: A New Psychology of Spiritual Optimism*. Thanks also to all the authors whose words I use as jumping-off points, and to the entire staff of Conari Press, who make this and all of our books happen. I consider it a great privilege to be able to create "books that make a difference" with you.

THE SIMPLE JOY OF LIVING FROM A GRATEFUL HEART

If you look to others for fulfillment,
you will never truly be fulfilled.
If your happiness depends on money,
you will never be happy with yourself.
Be content with what you have;
rejoice in the way things are.
When you realize there is nothing lacking,
the whole world belongs to you.

—Lao Tzu

YESTERDAY, WHILE PUTTING THE FINAL TOUCHES on this book, I went to lunch at a Chinese restaurant with my friend Annette to talk about gratitude. When I opened my fortune cookie at the end of the meal, the message was, "Stop searching happiness is just next to you." Talk about perfect timing! For that is exactly what this book is all about. Happiness, the sheer joy of being alive, is within our reach. All we need is an attitude of gratitude. Gratitude creates happiness because it makes us feel full, complete; gratitude is the realization that we have everything we need, at least in this moment.

There is a saying that people teach what they most need to learn, and nowhere is that more true than with me and gratitude. I wrote this book not only because I think gratitude is vitally important to our world, but because I want to become more consciously grateful myself. I do not set myself up as an "expert," but rather a person on a path like the rest of us, each of us becoming the fullness of who he or she is meant to be.

Like so many of us, I spent a great deal of my life, in my twenties and early thirties, cataloging all the ways I had been injured and abused. In therapy and out, with friends and loved ones, I analyzed and categorized the whos, whats, and wheres of my misery. I was a confirmed pessimist, always able to see the dark side of anything and everything. My belief was that life was hard and disaster was looming around every corner. If things were going well, it was only a matter of time before they would take a turn for the worse. Despite life's difficulties, it was my responsibility to do all the good I could and become the best person I could be. If I thought about gratitude at all, it was only to take a moment to give thanks for a few people in my life who had helped me feel loved.

Gradually, things changed for me. I can't point to a single event, a life-changing moment, when my attitudes suddenly transformed. Rather, slowly, as I came to understand my wounding better and began to heal, I started to notice the dearth of positive emotions in my life. I wasn't so miserable, worried, or alone anymore, but I knew precious little about joy, happiness, optimism, faith, and trust. So I began to study these emotions. (I always was a good student—give me something to study and I'll figure it out.)

I adopted certain people who seemed to naturally radiate happiness as my teachers of optimism and joyfulness. One of the things I noticed is that these people all had a profound sense of gratitude that seemed to flow uninhibitedly from them. Investigating further, I discovered that each of them had experienced at least as difficult an early life, if not more challenging, as I had. But my teachers consciously chose to adopt certain attitudes, such as gratitude, that led them to great happiness.

That's when I learned that you don't have to be saddled for life with the mental attitudes you adopted in early childhood. All of us are free to change our minds, and as we change our minds, our experiences will also change. So I set out on a course to be more grateful, joyful, and hopeful. The result of my course is what you are holding in your hands.

A few of my basic assumptions: I've learned over time that it helps to take the long view, to choose to see our lives from a spiritual perspective. I know we are here to "grow our souls," to heal our wounds—or at least bless our woundedness—and become more loving, kind, fearless, and hopeful. The longer I live, the more I recognize that cultivating an attitude of gratitude is the key to living from an open heart, that is, living in a spirit of joyful expectation.

Gratitude is not just the key. It's a magic key—all

you need to do is to use it, and the world is suddenly transformed into a beautiful wonderland, in which you are invited to play. That's because, like most of the great spiritual truths, gratitude is stunningly simple. This is not to say, however, that an attitude of gratitude is necessarily easy to practice. All kinds of distractions, obfuscation, and negative attitudes from our upbringings may get in the way. But all you really have to do is make a commitment to do it, and the magic will be yours.

One of the incredible truths about gratitude is that it is impossible to feel both the positive emotion of thankfulness and a negative emotion such as anger or fear at the same time. Gratitude births only positive feelings—love, compassion, joy, and hope. As we focus on what we are thankful for, fear, anger, and bitterness simply melt away, seemingly without effort.

How can this be? The answer is that gratitude helps us track success, to notice what is right in our lives, and the brain naturally works to track success. If you have ever watched a baby learn something, you'll know what I mean. Learning to walk, for example, she stands and puts out one foot. Boom! Down she goes because her balance wasn't right. Instead of castigating herself for blowing it, getting angry, or blaming the floor or her shoe, she just registers that it didn't work because her foot was too far out and tries again. She just keeps trying and trying, discarding what doesn't work without obsessing on it, and incorporating what's right until she can walk. Fall, fall, fall, walk, fall, fall, walk, walk, walk!

As we get older, however, we get schooled in our mistakes, and learn to focus on what's *not* right, what is lacking, missing, inadequate, and painful. That's why gratitude is so powerful. It helps us to return to our natural state of joyfulness where we notice what's right instead of what's wrong. Gratitude reminds us to be like plants, which turn toward, not away, from the light.

Because of the simple power of gratitude, it's easy to make all kinds of Pollyanna-ish generalities, which slide off into meaninglessness and are boring to read about. My hope is that within these pages you'll find true inspiration and some solid ideas for making the practice of living from a grateful heart real and meaningful.

To entice, encourage, and support you in your commitment, this little book begins with The Gifts of Gratitude, which look at what happens in our lives when we begin to practice gratitude. Don't worry if you don't know how to do it yet. Right now, we are focusing on the wonderful effects your new attitudes will create. We then go to The Attitudes of Gratitude, which are the outlooks or stances we need to take in cultivating gratefulness. Finally we move to The Practices of Gratitude, which are the practical ways we can develop and maintain thankfulness in our daily lives.

In a sense, each of the sixty chapters is a meditation in and of itself. This is not a book to be read at one sitting. Rather, I encourage you to read one chapter and let it sink in for a while—a day, two days, even a week or longer—before moving onto the next. Since gratitude is both an attitude and a practice, you need time to integrate the learnings so they can become truly yours, and not something you just read, put away, and forget.

To get started, take a few minutes right now to reflect on a happy moment in your own life that stands out for you, a moment that stays with you, even if it happened ten, twenty, or forty years ago. Experience it again: see the scene, hear the sounds that were around you, feel the sensations. What was it about that moment that stays with you? Was gratitude a part of it? What was going on for you that allowed you to feel grateful?

For me it is tiny kittens crawling down my back when I was about two. I can feel the tiny claws, hear their little mewls, and see the grey wispy baby fur. It is the prickle of the tiny claws against my skin—the sensation so deliciously startling—that makes me smile even now. It's the first memory I have of the wonder of being alive in a body. It was the newness, the "first ever-ness" that allowed me in that moment to feel grateful for being alive, and it is why that minute of my life continues to be one of my most powerful memories.

It has been a great joy for me to write this book, for its creation has been an act of gratitude in and of itself-for those who have so unselfishly taught and inspired me throughout my life; for those who shared specific ideas, stories, and practices with me; for my mind's ability to put it together; and for you, the reader, for being interested and willing to enter into the experience.

That's the most wonderful thing I've discovered so far about gratitude—it makes you feel full, bursting with delight, just to remember the gifts you have received. Thus are we doubly blessed when we receive something, for the gift itself, and later, in recall, for the miracle of having been given it.

THE GIFTS OF GRATITUDE

Gratitude unlocks the fullness of life.
It turns what we have into enough, and
more. It turns denial into acceptance,
chaos into order, confusion to clarity. . . .
Gratitude makes sense of our past, brings
peace for today, and creates a vision for
tomorrow.

—Melody Beattie

CONSCIOUSLY CULTIVATING THANKFULNESS is a journey of the soul, one that begins when we look around us and see the positive effects that gratitude creates. We do this by noticing those around us to whom gratefulness comes easily and realize how much we enjoy being around these people. We also tap into these gifts as we think about times in the past when we felt particularly grateful. Remember the peacefulness and the delight that accompanied those times? As we come to understand the gifts of gratitude, we realize that being grateful is not something remote or foreign, but part of the natural joyful expression of our full humanness.

Gratitude Is the Mother of Joy

*Joy is prayer—Joy is strength—Joy is love—Joy
is a net of love by which you can catch souls.
She gives most who gives with joy.*

—MOTHER TERESA

I don't know about you, but in general, there hasn't
been a lot of joy, that opening and swelling of the
heart, in my life. It wasn't because of my circumstances,
because they weren't particularly hard, but because of
my mental training. Growing up, I learned to plan and
to work hard. Accomplishments were good because
they led somewhere I was planning to go: high school,
college, a good job, a relationship. But they weren't to
be relished and celebrated in and of themselves.

Like so many of us, I was so busy climbing the ladder of success, that I took no time to enjoy the journey.
I was too busy getting on to the next challenge. When
I think back on particular occasions for joy in my past—
graduating valedictorian of my high school, getting
married, making a bestseller list for *Random Acts of
Kindness*, for example—I realize that as soon as I attained
each goal, my eyes were immediately on the next
"prize": getting to the top of my college class, having a

baby, getting on the *New York Times* bestseller list. It was as if I was a machine, mindlessly churning out accomplishments and not stopping to relish the journey along the way.

But I got sick and tired of a joyless existence, and so have thought a lot in the past few years about how to bring more joy into my life. The more I think about it, the more I believe that joy and gratitude are inseparable. *Joy* is defined in the dictionary as an "emotion evoked by well-being, success, or good fortune or by the prospect of possessing what one desires," while *gratitude* is that "state of being appreciative of benefits received." In other words, whenever we are appreciative, we are filled with a sense of well-being and swept up by the feeling of joy.

So I determined to stop climbing mindlessly to some undefined peak of accomplishment and focus my attention on all the wonderful things that were happening in my day-to-day existence. As I do, without my even trying, joy creeps in.

How about you? As Sarah Ban Breathnach puts it, "Begin today. Declare out loud to the Universe that you are willing to let go of struggle and eager to learn through joy." Then think of all that you have accomplished today and celebrate each feat, no matter its size.

Gratitude Makes Us Young

The invariable mark of wisdom is to see
the miraculous in the common.

—RALPH WALDO EMERSON

Young children are such exuberant, joy-filled creatures, eager to embrace life in all its mystery and
majesty. Everything is new and exciting; everything—a
bubble, a snowflake, a mud puddle—is a gift. But something in the process of growing up so often takes the
juice out of us. We become encrusted, hard, jaded. We
lose our joy, our exuberance, our passionate embrace of
life. We trudge instead of skip, retreat instead of
explore, "too old for that," whatever "that" is.

This drying up is so common that when we meet a
vibrant, joy-filled older person, he or she stands out as a
singular exception. But we don't have to lose the happiness or juiciness of youth. All we need to do is to tap
into our sense of gratitude, for when we do, we are like
little children again, seeing the world for the first time.

In *Simple Pleasures of the Garden*, Dawna Markova shares
a story about such a woman: "Several years ago, I was
walking in March along a gravel road that led to the
ocean in Rhode Island. A very old and thin woman came

hobbling down a driveway toward me. I waved and continued walking, but as I passed, she grabbed my arm, turned around and began to pull me in the direction of her house. I instantly thought of the witch in *Hansel and Gretel*, and tried to pull back, but that only made her clutch tighter around my wrist. Besides, she didn't cackle, so I relented.

"She didn't say a word, in fact, until we approached her house: a shingle-style cottage with green shutters and a front lawn erupting everywhere in purple crocus. She released me there, throwing her arms up in the air and shouting, 'Look at this splendor! Isn't it a miracle?!'"

This old woman was open to the magic and beauty of life, and her sparkling eyes and eagerness to share made her and everything around her more vibrant and alive.

Attitudes of gratitude

Gratitude Makes Us Feel Good

*Mental sunshine will cause the flowers of peace,
happiness, and prosperity to grow upon the face of
the Earth. Be a creator of mental sunshine.*

—GRAFFITI ON A WALL IN BERKELEY, CALIFORNIA

Tom comes from a family of highly successful businesspeople who taught him to climb the ladder of success by criticizing him whenever he did something wrong. He learned early on that life is "hard work," that it's a "dog-eat-dog world," and that to get ahead he had to never make a mistake. While he did succeed, including getting an M.B.A. from a top business school, he was never happy. To him, work seemed only drudgery; he spent much of his time noticing what he did wrong: he didn't assert himself at the meeting, he should have made more calls. Most of the time he felt lifeless and depressed.

Finally Tom went to a therapist to ask for a prescription for Prozac. But since he really didn't want to take an antidepressant if he didn't have to, at the therapist's suggestion, he agreed to first try something else for one month. Before he started work in the morning, he was to ask himself, "What do I feel grateful for about myself?" In this way, he reminded himself of his resources, strengths, and talents. Then, at the end of the day, he was to finish work by asking, "What did I do today that I feel good about?"

"Do you know what I discovered?" he told me. "Gratitude is a natural upper. It works so well that now, whenever I feel my energy going down during the day, I ask myself, what do I feel grateful for in this moment?" By concentrating on what he's doing right and what he appreciates about himself, Tom overcame his depression and has begun to look forward to work.

Gratitude makes us feel good because it helps us widen our frame of vision. Under depression or stress, we can develop tunnel vision, seeing only this problem, that difficulty. We can get overtaken by a heavy, dark feeling of despair. But when we experience a sense of gratitude, we give ourselves a dose of mental sunshine. Suddenly the world seems brighter, and we have more options.

And the greatest thing is that as we experience the mental sunshine of gratitude, we begin to glow with sunshine ourselves. Suddenly not only is the world brighter, but we are too. Soon we notice that our lives are full of people who want to be around us because we exude peacefulness, happiness, and joy.

Gratitude Promotes Health

Feelings of gratitude release positive endorphins
throughout the body, creating health.

—SHARON HUFFMAN

Josephine is a seventy-seven-year-old woman who, in her late fifties, was diagnosed with a malignant brain tumor and scheduled for surgery a few days later. While waiting for the operation, she sat in her porch swing and gave thanks for all the wonderful things in her life. She wrote a letter of thanks to each of her family members, called them around her, and went into the hospital. The night before surgery, she suddenly saw "what looked like a beautiful woman with long, flowing hair smiling at me and radiating light. She said she was an angel who felt my love and she had come to reassure me that everything was OK; that I would have plenty of time to fulfill my life's purpose. And then she said, 'Always remember that it was your love and your appreciation that brought healing to you.'" It turned out that the tumor was gone, and Josephine was sent home without surgery.

Not all healings are as miraculous as Josephine's, but recent scientific research has begun to indicate that positive emotions, such as gratitude and love, have beneficial effects on health. They do so by strengthening and enhancing the immune system, which enables the body to resist disease and recover more quickly from illness, through the release of endorphins into the bloodstream. Endorphins are the body's natural painkillers. Among other effects, they stimulate dilation of the blood vessels, which leads to a relaxed heart.

Conversely, negative emotions such as worry, anger, and hopelessness reduce the number and slow down the movement of disease-fighting white cells in our bloodstreams, and contribute to the development of stroke and heart disease by dumping high levels of adrenaline into the bloodstream. Adrenaline constricts blood vessels, particularly to the heart, raising blood pressure and potentially damaging arteries and the heart itself.

What this means is that the more we experience a sense of gratitude, the more endorphins and the less adrenaline we pump into our systems, thus contributing to longer, healthier lives. As we count our blessings, we literally bathe ourselves inwardly in good hormones. And while we can't guarantee that a sense of appreciation will cure us as it did Josephine, we *can* be sure that it will make us feel better!

Gratitude Eradicates Worry

You cannot be grateful and unhappy at the same time.
—A WOMAN TO DR. TOM COSTA

If worrying were a paying job, I would be a rich woman. Somehow during my childhood, I got the idea that worrying could actually stave off future disaster, and as I entered adulthood, I became convinced that if I were to stop worrying, took my eye off the ball, as it were, that something dreadful would happen. If I worried enough about being poor, I wouldn't be. If I worried enough about my partner's safety, nothing would happen to him. If I worried enough about my stepson's health, he wouldn't get sick. There was no room in my heart for happiness because worry took up all the space. (Indeed I was convinced that if I were too happy, it would somehow hex the situation. If I got too happy about love, for example, I wouldn't worry sufficiently and therefore it would be taken from me.)

In my forties, I have been working on letting go of my compulsive worrying, and I have been amazed at how swiftly a sense of gratefulness banishes the worry warts. And I've tried many other things—asking myself what is the worst thing that could happen and imagining going through that to a new place; noticing without judgment my worry; indulging it; pushing it away. None of these has been as effective as tapping into a sense of appreciation *in this moment* for what I do have.

Worried about money? I focus on the fact that so far, I have always had what I needed and right now, I have enough. Worried about health? I focus on the amount of good health I'm thankful to be experiencing right now. Worried about—my favorite—a loved one being taken suddenly in an accident? I focus on how grateful I am that they are in my life right now.

I think tapping into the wellspring of gratitude works for two reasons. First, worry is always about the future, if only the next hour or minute, whereas gratitude is in the here and now. Cast over your list of worries. Aren't they always about what might or might not happen? You are worried about the reaction of your boss tomorrow to your presentation. You're worried about how you are going to afford to send your son to college. You're worried about the test results. In every case, you project yourself into the future and imagine something bad happening. As André Dubus points out, "It is not hard to live through a day if you can live through a moment. What creates despair is the imagination, which pretends there is a future and insists on predicting millions of moments, thousands of days, and so drains you that you cannot live the moment at hand." Gratitude brings you back to the present moment, to all that is working perfectly right now. Tomorrow may bring difficulties, but for right now, things are pretty good.

Gratefulness also eliminates worry because it reminds us of the abundance of our universe. Yes, something bad might happen, but given all that you have received so far, chances are you will continue to be supported on your journey through life, even in ways you would never have guessed or chosen for yourself.

23

Gratitude Draws People to Us

*Sometimes I go about with pity for
myself and all the while Great Winds are
carrying me across the sky.*

—OJIBWAY SAYING

I have a friend who can't seem to find one good thing about her life. She complains constantly about her job, her coworkers, and her relationships with men. She puts herself down a good bit, too. It does no good whatsoever for me to point out all the good things that I see in her life. It just starts another round of "poor me." After I spend an afternoon with her, I feel cranky, depressed, and, frankly, bored. I notice that I try to avoid getting together with her.

The opposite is true about my friend Abby. Abby has had a hard life, too. She wasn't born into a wealthy family; she has raised a son by herself, put herself through college, and taken care of aged and ill relatives. But she is cheerful and upbeat most of the time, and I love being around her, because when we're together, life seems easy and joyful.

Recently, I made the observation that she had a great career and seemed to be appreciated by her boss and company. She replied, "Oh, yes! I love my job and I'm lucky to have it. Every morning when I drive to work, I grab the steering wheel and thank God for my job. For the job that paid for this nice car I wouldn't have otherwise, for the nice people I work with in a beautiful office and for a boss that treats me and everyone else so well. I'm absolutely grateful for what I have and make a point to give thanks on my way to work. It grounds me and starts off day on a positive note that carries me along on wings!"

I am convinced that it is Abby's sense of gratitude that gives her such an upbeat attitude. It's also why, I believe, she has more friends than anyone else I know. For when we are grateful, we exude happiness and that makes us magnets that draw other people toward us. They want to be around that exuberant energy.

Gratitude not only draws people to us, but it helps us keep those who are in our sphere. When we see the glass as half-full, rather than half-empty, we notice what is there rather than dwelling on what is not. When we notice what's there, we get out of our self-absorption and realize that there *are* people around us, many of whom have done wonderful things for us. And when we express our gratitude for their presence in our lives, it's more likely that those people will want to continue to be around us.

Gratitude Is the Antidote to Bitterness and Resentment

The more light you allow within you, the brighter the world you live in will be.

—SHAKTI GAWAIN

Twenty years ago, Cynthia, a petite, talented woman in her late twenties, got divorced in a terrible breakup. Two decades later, bitter and resentful, she is still obsessed with her ex-husband, bad-mouthing him to her children and friends whenever she gets a chance, convinced that he ruined her life. In a way, of course, he did. Because she kept focusing on her pain and resentment, she was never able to heal and move on. Hurt and hateful, she hasn't been able to attract new love in her life, and her now-grown children avoid her like the plague.

Have you ever met someone so bitter about their life that they feel like a black hole sucking away all the energy around them? Whether we call them pessimists, ingrates, or those who always see the glass as half-empty, they are a drag to be around. So focused on what hasn't worked for them they can't see the ways they have been the recipients of gifts, blessings, and surprises.

Most of us aren't total black holes, but when we fail to give thanks for what happens in our lives, we can get hung up in bitterness that prevents us from developing emotionally and spiritually. If we fail to grow, the light inside us grows dim.

Bitterness is a poison that snuffs the light of our souls, hardening us to life's pleasures and joys by keeping us focused only on what is wrong. When the man I lived with for fourteen years left me, he said it was because I was turning bitter and he didn't want to stick around to see it. Although there were other reasons for our breakup, including many he was responsible for, after the pain of the loss had subsided I gave thanks to him for the wake-up call; I *was* turning into a resentful woman, and that was the last thing on Earth I wanted to be.

I'm determined not to sink into bitterness again. While there are plenty of things in life to be justifiably annoyed, angry, or hurt at, that doesn't mean that I should completely ignore all that is beautiful, good, and touching. I want my soul to shine with an overflowing of love, and practicing gratitude is one of the best ways I know to do it.

Gratitude is a inner light that we can use to illumine our souls. The more we are thankful, the more light we experience and the more we shine forth into the world.

Gratitude Cures Perfectionism

*A point worth pondering: Upon completing the
Universe, the Great Creator pronounced
it "very good." Not "perfect."*

—SARAH BAN BREATHNACH

When I was young, I wanted to be a saint. Not just plain old good, but a bona fide canonized saint. I figured that anything worth doing was worth doing perfectly, and while I was being perfect, I might as well get all the adoration that perfectionism deserves. Sainthood seemed to fit the bill. Unfortunately, I kept slipping up: I would forget to make my bed or get jealous of my little brother, and then sink into despair, convinced I was a complete failure.

Ah, perfectionism! Those of us afflicted with the pesky bug may look with amazement (You mean you don't care you didn't do it perfectly??) or disdain (What kind of lazy, good-for-nothing guy *are* you?) upon those who don't suffer from it, but the truth, of course, is that it springs from our own sense of lack. We simply don't believe we're good enough as we are in our humble, human, imperfect state, and must therefore compensate by being Miss Perfect Goody-Two-Shoes.

That was certainly true for me. Somehow, as a child, I got the message that if only I did everything perfectly, life would be OK. But life has a way of being messy and imperfectable, despite our best efforts, and individuals, including myself, are equally incapable of perfection. After decades of being a wannabe saint, I finally got worn out from trying. Now, instead of attempting to make everyone and everything fit my plan (an impossible task, even for a saint), I spend the energy I used to pour into sainthood school to be more grateful.

Because perfectionism is born of a sense of inadequacy, of lack, an attitude of gratitude counteracts it by tapping us into the experience of abundance. Gratitude makes our world feel complete and right. When we feel the fullness of gratitude, we accept life just as it is— however messy, complicated, and drawn-outside-the-lines that may be.

Gratitude not only helps us accept that the world is imperfect, but that we are too—and that's OK. For when we pour the oil of appreciation for life in all its

imperfections over our experience, we ourselves can't help but be anointed. Suddenly seized by joy for the crazy, mixed-up world, we recognize ourselves as part of that world, and take our rightful place as a child of the Universe, perfectly acceptable in all our imperfection.

Gratitude Releases Us from the "Gimmes"

If there is to be any peace it will come through being, not having.

—HENRY MILLER

A few years ago, I noticed that if a weekend went by without my buying something other than food for the week, I got an itchy feeling. I wanted to shop, to buy, to consume—it didn't matter what. I didn't actually need anything, but I wanted to purchase *something*.

I don't think I was alone in the feeling. Consumer debt is at the highest level in U.S. history, as are personal bankruptcies. We're literally buying ourselves into financial holes too large for many of us to crawl out of.

I didn't like feeling that I was a slave to shopping. So I decided to buy less and appreciate what I already had more. Instead of a new blouse, I wore an old favorite. But instead of just putting it on mindlessly, I tried really noticing what I liked about it: the delicate embroidery, the silky feel of the satin, the vibrant shade of red. That's when I discovered one of the greatest gifts of gratitude—it gets us off the consuming treadmill so many of us are caught on. Here's how.

A perennial dieting tip is to eat something and then wait twenty minutes before deciding to eat something again. The reason is that your body needs that much time to register that it is full. If you keep eating without pausing, you will not realize that your body is full, and therefore you may overeat.

Giving thanks for what we have in our lives is like that pause when eating. It allows us to feel full, to register on the emotional and spiritual level that we have, in fact, been given "enough." If we don't practice gratitude on a daily basis, it's easy to overconsume, to feel a lack and to try to fill that lack through possessions, because on a psychological level we haven't registered that we already have what we need.

I've spent years talking about this to people, but the only way to really get it is to try it yourself. For two weeks, don't buy anything new except food. Try really to take in the gifts you already have, not just the wonderful intangible ones such as good health or love in your life, but the material ones as well—your cozy apartment, the green pitcher your mother gave you, the gargoyle bookends, your favorite earrings. Walk around where you live and really notice and give thanks for the objects in your life that give you joy. Then notice what effect it has on your desire to buy more.

Gratitude Keeps Us Current

That it will never come again is
what makes life so sweet.
—EMILY DICKINSON

L ast night I watched my daughter Ana, whom we
recently adopted from China, lie on the bed in an
ecstatic trance of bottle-sucking. Her eyes closed, her
rosebud mouth pursed, her exquisitely long fingers
curled around the plastic bottle, she gave herself over
to the experience. She wasn't obsessing on past
wounds, although perhaps she had a right to.
Neglected for over a year, when we got her she had
second-degree burns on her buttocks from lying in
urine. Nor was she worrying about where future bottles
might come from, although she had a right to do that
also. Abandoned on Christmas evening on a cold street
until someone heard her newborn cries, she had been
fed only watered-down milk and seemed to be starving
the first few weeks we fed her.

Rather, she was so focused on appreciating the warm
milk as it went down her throat that everything else,
past and future, simply disappeared. As I looked at her,
I realized that this total and complete absorption in the

present moment is available to us all when we choose to let gratitude wash over us uninhibitedly.

But many of us have been taught not to give ourselves over so fully to something or someone. As a child, I believed that you couldn't let yourself become totally immersed in an experience, because something bad might be happening as your attention is diverted. My parents used to say that as a child they never saw me asleep; I always had one eye open, alert to disaster.

But if Ana, who has suffered so much in her very short life, can give herself over to the joy of completely appreciating her bottle, can't I allow myself in this moment to fully appreciate the sweet peas on my desk, the wonder of being able to think and read and write?

As I allow myself to open to the fullness of gratitude, the past and future fade away and I become more alive in the present moment. That's because gratitude is, for the most part, about the here and now. While we can be thankful for past blessings and hope for future ones, when we experience a sense of gratefulness, we are usually contemplating some present circumstance. We are brought up to date with ourselves. Our focus moves away from all that we or others did or failed to do in the past, or what we hope for or worry about in the future, and we find ourselves placed squarely in this precious moment, this experience that will never happen again.

Gratitude Opens Our Hearts

The most invisible creators I know of are those
artists whose medium is life itself. The ones who express
the inexpressible—without brush, hammer, clay or guitar.
They neither paint nor sculpt—their medium is their
being. Whatever their presence touches has increased life.
They see and don't have to draw. They are
the artists of being alive.

—J. STONE

I spent several Christmases recently with a family that loves to give presents. Every year, the floor around the tree was heaped with hundreds of gifts, so many that it took the entire morning to open them all. But despite all that was given and received, I would leave there every year feeling empty and alone. There had been a plethora of presents, but no presence. This family gave so many gifts because they didn't know how to connect deeply to themselves and one another. They ripped through the mounds of merchandise, saying a pro forma "Thank you," but no sense of true appreciation was expressed or received.

The experience was so powerful—the contrast

between the material plenty and the emotional lack—it set me to thinking. That's when I realized that you can't experience gratitude with a closed heart. It's just not possible. Gratefulness is only experienced in the moments in which we open our hearts to life—to the beauty in this moment, to the possibility of surprise in the next.

A person does something kind for you, even a very small thing, say, holding a door open for you. When you say, "Thank you" *and really mean it,* rather than saying it out of social convention, your heart instinctively opens to the person. In that moment, you experience your connection to one another, even if you never lay eyes on each other again.

Openheartedness takes courage. It requires enough trust in the goodness of other people and the universe at large that we can put aside our self-protectiveness—that stance that says I am not going to be grateful for what I am receiving right now because it's too scary to risk getting hurt—and take a leap of faith to acknowledge that we have received a gift.

The fact that true gratitude creates a sense of openheartedness is the reason so much of the "thanks" in this culture is rote and unfeeling. People are afraid to feel thankful, because they are afraid of the out-of-control experience that occurs when they acknowledge the bond between giver and receiver. We are afraid to feel the love that gets created any time we express true thanks. As adults, our hearts have been broken many times and, by golly, we want to make sure it doesn't happen again.

The choice is ours, in every moment. Do we want to live in seeming safety, shut inside the shell of our individuality, unwilling to experience the deep and abiding connections that are ours in any case, or are we willing to risk, over and over, having our hearts broken open to the beauty and the pain of all that is ours to experience?

When do you experience an open heart? What are the conditions that foster your willingness to open your heart? As we practice true gratitude, we learn to take the risk over and over again.

37

Gratitude Spawns Kindness and Generosity

Our work-a-day lives are filled with opportunities to bless others. The power of a single glance or an encouraging smile must never be underestimated.

—G. RICHARD RIEGER

Deborah Chamberin-Taylor had been studying Buddhism in Thailand, at a monastery where all the teaching, housing, and meals were free. Shortly before she left, a Thai family came and made a meal for the 250 retreatants as a way of expressing their gratitude for the teachings of the Buddha.

Shortly thereafter, Deborah was helping to plan a weekend retreat in Northern California. The planning group was discussing how to feed lunch to all those who would be attending, because the cost of the meal was not in the budget. Filled with a sense of gratitude for the generosity of the Thai family, Deborah found herself volunteering to pay for lunch for all the participants. "I noticed what joy it brought me to consider giving such a gift.... Later, when I told this story to a group, I was pleasantly surprised when person after person walked up and handed me unsolicited money for the 'lunch fund.' They also wanted to be part of fueling the 'cycle of generosity.'"

As this Deborah's story shows, gratitude begets generosity which begets gratitude which begets generosity. Gratitude creates a sense of fullness; it is, in fact, the very sense of fullness. And from this fullness, we feel moved to give. That's because true kindness and generosity come from a response to this sense of fullness: we give best from overflow.

It's a beautiful cycle. The more you feel grateful, the stronger is the impulse toward giving. And the more you give, the more you get—love, friendship, a sense of purpose and accomplishment, even, sometimes, material wealth. As author Lewis Smedes notes, "When I feel the joy of receiving a gift my heart nudges me to join creation's ballet, the airy dance of giving and receiving, and getting and giving again."

It doesn't have to be an extravagant, expensive gift. When we live with a grateful heart, we will see endless opportunities to give: a flower from the garden to a coworker, a kind word to our child, a visit to an old person. You will know what to do.

Gratitude Joins Us to All Life

I feel this communion, this strange attunement,
most readily with large white pines, a little less with sugar
maples, beeches, or oaks. Clearly white pines and I are on
the same wave-length. What I give back to the trees I
cannot imagine. I hope they receive something,
because trees are among my closest friends.

—ANNE LABASTILLE

I n *The Continuum Concept,* Jean Liedloff describes a profound experience she had when she was eight years
old of the connection that Anne Labastille describes.
"The incident happened during a nature walk in the
Maine woods where I was at summer camp. I was last in
line; I had fallen back a bit and was hurrying to catch up
when, through the trees, I saw a glade. It had a lush fir
tree at the far side and a knoll in the center covered in
bright, almost luminous green moss. The rays of the
afternoon sun slanted against the blue-black green of the
pine forest. The little roof of visible sky was perfectly
blue. The whole picture had a completeness, an all-there
quality of such dense power that it stopped me in my
tracks. . . . Everything was in its place—the tree, the earth

underneath, the rock, the moss. In autumn it would be right; in winter under the snow, it would be perfect in its wintriness. Spring would come again and miracle within miracle would unfold, each at its special pace, some things having died off, some sprouting in their first spring, but all of equal and utter rightness....

"That night in my camp bed I brought The Glade to mind and was filled with a sense of thankfulness, and renewed my vow to preserve my vision."

"With every leaf a miracle..." writes Walt Whitman in his poetic tribute to lilacs, and this is what he is talking about—when we are in touch with a profound sense of gratitude, we connect to *all* of life, recognizing the miracle in the tallest tree, the smallest bug.

Such a sense of connection is purely joyful; it grants to our human endeavors no more or less importance than they should have, and inspires us to do whatever we can to conserve and protect all of the natural wonders of the Earth and sea, not just those that are convenient for us. Thus gratitude also gives birth to a fiercely loving environmentalism, a sensitivity born of the connection made explicit between us and everything else that creeps, crawls, sways, and clings. We recognize that we cannot live outside of the great web of life that lovingly holds us in its nurturing embrace, and we vow to protect the sanctity of that web.

Gratitude Connects Us to Spirit

*If the only prayer you say in your whole life
is "thank you," that would suffice.*

—MEISTER ECKHART

Marjory is a former "jeweler to the stars" who made one-of-a-kind rings and other extraordinary pieces for such luminaries as Tina Turner. Her business boomed and the good times did indeed roll. When gold prices skyrocketed, however, her business went bust and she became a recluse in a small cabin. But she refused to feel sorry for herself.

On a flight during a recent job-hunting trip, Marjory was seated by Paul, a charming and sweet Baptist teenager from South Carolina on his way to China. Now, it's easy to figure out within a couple of minutes of meeting Marjory that her religious leanings are fairly New Age, especially as she goes over her complete astrological chart with you right off the bat! In any case, the two were chatting away when Marjory noticed the spectacular sunset diffusing golden and fuchsia light, turning the Pacific Ocean into a pool of amber glass. "Oh, God. Look at that. How beautiful!" Marjory exclaimed, her eyes tearing over.

Paul, turned to Marjory gravely and asked, "Who is your God?"

Taken aback, Marjory replied that her God was just God and she didn't worry much about where he came from. The teen pressed to know if her God was the Father of his personal Savior, Jesus Christ. Marjory stared back, glassy-eyed, when a small miracle took place.

Paul began quoting from Psalm 23, a magnificent and lyrical stream of biblical poetry about how beautiful this home is that God had made for us. Marjory and everyone else within earshot relaxed instantly and looked at the sunset, seeing again, through the eyes of timeless wonder and gratitude, the marvel of this world we live in.

However you experience God—as loving Father, nurturing Mother, Creator of all that is, your Higher Power, the Spirit of Kindness and Compassion, whatever is true for you—the quickest, easiest way to connect to Him/Her/It is to express your gratitude. That's because gratitude is the response to the giver of a gift—and when we give thanks for things beyond the gifts, we receive from other people, we are de facto thanking the Greater Power for what we have received: food, shelter, the beautiful sunny day, life itself. As we give thanks, our spirits join with the Great Spirit in the dance of life that is the interplay between giver and receiver.

I love the sensibility of this exchange that is inherent in Native American spirituality. Whenever a person is about to take the life of something—a deer, a tree—he or she humbly asks permission of the Spirit that dwells in the animal or plant, and gives thanks for their willingness to sacrifice their own life. Sometimes, an offering, such as a pinch of corn or tobacco, is given in compensation. Such an act acknowledges that something has been given and received on both sides.

45

THE GIFTS OF
GRATITUDE

Gratitude Opens Us to Moments of Grace

Nobody can conceive or imagine all the wonders there are unseen and unseeable in the world.

—FRANCIS P. CHURCH

Morihei Ueshiba, the father of Aikido, once described an experience he had walking alone in his garden. Suddenly "I felt that a golden spirit sprang up from the ground.... My mind and body turned into light. I was able to understand the whispering of the birds, and was clearly aware of the mind of God ... the spirit of loving protection for all beings. Endless tears of joy streamed down my cheeks. Since that time, I have grown to feel that the whole earth is my house...."

Have you ever had an experience in which you slip out of ordinary space and time and tap into the flow of the universe, where there is no separation between you and everything else and where everything seems perfectly right just as it is? Some people find such moments of transcendence through meditation, others in nature, still others when making love. As a young child, I often experienced such moments in the early spring tromping alone in the icy stream near my house.

Such moments are rare gifts, in which we open to an expansive, ecstatic state of Big Mind, the place where all is right with us and the world. These moments of grace are so rare and so wonderful that many spiritual seekers spend a lifetime trying to experience them. And the desire to feel such expansiveness is often the impetus for taking mind-altering drugs.

I'm convinced that you don't have to meditate for years on a mountaintop or take LSD to experience such transcendence. All you have to do is tap into the fullness of a sense of gratitude, and grace will likely descend. (Indeed, I am sure that what meditation and mind-altering drugs do is break down the barriers to experiencing gratitude in its full abundance.)

We can't force or demand such magical mystical experiences. But we can offer ourselves up as willing and worthy participants by reveling in the wonders that we are already experiencing. Through gratitude, our souls, in Emily Dickinson's words, "always stand ajar; ready to welcome the ecstatic experience."

THE ATTITUDES OF GRATITUDE

*The most powerful agent of growth
and transformation is something much
more basic than any technique: a
change of heart.*

—JOHN WELWOOD

THE NEXT STEP ON THE JOURNEY is to look at the attitudes of gratitude—those beliefs that foster a sense of thankfulness. Attitudes are the underpinnings of action; as John Welwood implies, we can't change on the outside until and unless we transform our thinking, transform the way we imagine ourselves and our reality. The good news is that we really *can* decide to see the glass as half-full rather than half-empty, and that decision will have profoundly positive effects not only on our happiness and that of those around us, but on the way our whole lives unfold.

Life Is a Miracle

*The Zen master Ling Chi said that the miracle is not
to walk on burning charcoal or in the thin air or on the
water; the miracle is just to walk on earth. You breathe in.
You become aware of the fact that you are alive. You are
still alive and you are walking on this beautiful planet. . . .
The greatest of all miracles is to be alive.*

—THICH NHAT HANH

Thich Nhat Hanh is a Vietnamese Buddhist monk
who now lives in exile in France. While living in
Vietnam, he endured all kinds of hardships, including
the killings by either the French, American, or
Vietnamese military of family members and friends. An
orphanage that he started was bombed. And yet he is a
walking example of joy and gratitude. When asked how
he survived such difficulties with such peace and love in
his heart, he replied that every morning he used to ask
himself what he could count on that day; sometimes it
was only the blue sky and the brown earth, and the fact
that he was still breathing in and out. But in counting his
blessings, so to speak, he reconnected to the miracle
that he was, at least for the present moment, still alive in

this beautiful world. "Suffering is not enough. Life is both dreadful and wonderful," he reminds us. "How can I smile when I am filled with so much sorrow? It is natural—you need to smile to your sorrow because you are more than your sorrow."

Buddhist and Sufi teachers spend a lot of time talking about "waking up," by which they mean, I think, living life to its fullest because we are aware of living it moment to moment. Aware of breathing in, aware of breathing out; aware of chewing and swallowing our food; aware of placing one foot in front of the other when walking. Aware of seeing your infant son, of the effect of your words on a coworker, of the fact that your one foot is resting on top of the other.

Spiritual leaders teach that waking up is a process, that it doesn't just happen once and for all, but must occur again and again when we realize we have forgotten the miracle of being alive, and in recognizing our forgetfulness, we wake to the miracle once again. In the moments we are awake to the wonder of simply being alive, gratitude flows, no matter our circumstances.

When times have been tough for me, I have done a similar practice to Thich Nhat Hanh's. Before getting up in the morning, I have asked myself what I could count on that day, both externally—that I still had a place to live and food on the table; and internally—the deep love and trust, for example, that I feel for my friends.

It's a wonderful antidote to worry and opens you to gratitude, provided that you really stick to what you can count on today. Sometimes I would find myself, for instance, when I thought about the fact that I had a house, saying, "Yes, but I don't know if I can afford it tomorrow and what if the earthquake strikes, and.... " Then I would choose to stop and say, "This is just for today. What can you count on today?" As we learn how to appreciate the miracle of being alive, we will find the peace and the strength to face life's challenges as they come.

53

The Universe Is Friendly

*Einstein was asked what he thought the most important
question was that a human being needed to answer.
His reply was "Is the universe friendly or not?"*

—JOAN BORYSENKO

For most of my life, I have subscribed to the "Watch
out—disaster might strike at any time, so don't get
too complacent" school. It probably comes as no surprise that I have suffered from chronic muscle spasms in
my back and neck my whole life; even my body is per-
petually tensed for trouble. By age forty-four, I was just
plain sick of it, tired of waiting for the boom to fall, tired
of clenching in fear rather than opening in expectation.
So I decided to live as if the universe were friendly.

I have been meditating on Einstein's question for
over a year now, and I am convinced that how each of
us answers it is the key to whether we are happy and
joy-filled or not, and whether or not an attitude of gratitude comes easily. If we believe the universe is friendly,
then we believe that life is on our side, that good things
will come our way; and that even when bad things happen, they are bumps in the road designed to teach us to
become more wise, more whole, more loving. In this

view of the universe, gratitude flows from us naturally, as an instinctive response to the bounty we perceive all around us.

If, on the other hand, we believe the universe is unfriendly, then we see our life as an endless struggle against difficult odds, we believe that bad things are either random or sent purposely to torture us, that there is nothing we can count on and therefore we must brace ourselves for the next crisis, hoarding what we have. In this view, gratitude is very situation-specific. We're grateful— maybe—when things go well, but we are always ready for the boom to fall and for it all to disappear.

I have lapses in believing in the friendly universe, particularly when things are going badly money-wise. When I forget, I take out a piece of paper on which I've copied down a piece of an Inuit teaching: "The inhabitant or soul of the universe is never seen; its voice alone is heard. All we know is that it has a gentle voice, like a woman a voice so fine ... that even children cannot become afraid. And what it says is '*Sila ersinarsinivdluge,*' 'Be not afraid of the universe.'" It helps me remember that if I place my trust in the beneficence of the universe, things tend to work out. And if they don't, at least in the meantime I will enjoy myself a whole lot more and be more fun to be around.

ℒet Gratitude Flow Naturally

One's destination is never a place but rather
a new way of looking at things.
—HENRY MILLER

Nothing destroys a sense of gratitude faster than being told we "should" feel grateful. Some "should"s are necessary: in teaching manners to children (children learn not only by example, but by pairing instruction to example). But when we try to experience gratitude as a living force in our lives, guilt, whether imposed by others or by ourselves, is deadly.

We've probably all had someone in our lives tell us we should be grateful for something, or perhaps we say it to ourselves. Either way, this is the least likely way to promote an attitude of gratitude. As far as I can tell, gratitude is generated in two ways: one, by a spontaneous upswelling of the heart toward the wonder of life and all its particulars; and two, by a conscious decision to practice looking at what's right in our lives rather than focusing on what's missing. Either way, we don't get to gratitude by guilt-trips.

Guilt is a terrible motivator. It makes us want to run

away from whatever is making us feel bad, and to avoid looking at whatever is underlying it.

I say this because I don't want you, after reading this book, to go away thinking you "should" feel grateful. I want to encourage us all to open our hearts and experience gratitude as much as we can. But I know for myself that there are days when it is impossible for me to feel thankful for *anything* no matter how hard I try—and if that's true for you sometimes, be gentle with yourself. The more you allow what is true for you to be true, and the less you "should" yourself, the more space you create for the possibility of gratitude to quietly, softly enter your heart.

*Attitudes of
gratitude*

The Flashlight in Your Own Back Yard

Inside yourself or outside, you never have to change
what you see, only the way you see it.

—THADDEUS GOLAS

I went to see my father in the hospital about a week before he died. He had suffered for years with emphysema, hooked up to an oxygen tank, barely able to move around, and was failing fast. Bedridden, he was on constant oxygen and medication; his six-foot-two frame weighed only 130 pounds because eating anything but ice cream was too difficult. Every breath was a labored struggle. I asked him whether the quality of his life was worth all the effort. "I still enjoy being alive," he responded. "Sometimes it's easier to breathe and then I really enjoy just quietly taking a breath. I still enjoy reading the comics in the newspaper and watching the ball games on TV. My life is good." He said not a word about all that he had lost, all that he would never do again.

When I was about to do publicity for *A Grateful Heart*, I talked to my friend Dawna Markova about how to speak about the power of gratitude. She's great at metaphors, which are wonderful ways to look at things from a new perspective. What she said I have carried with me ever since: "Gratitude is like a flashlight. If you go out in your yard at night and turn on a flashlight, you suddenly can see what's there. It was always there, but you couldn't see it in the dark."

Exactly! Gratitude lights up what is already there. You don't necessarily have anything more or different, but suddenly you can actually see what is. And because you can see, you no longer take it for granted. You're just standing in your yard, but suddenly you realize, Oh, there's the first flower of spring struggling to emerge from the snow; Oh, there's a deer emerging from the scrub brush; Oh, there's the measuring cup you've been looking for that your daughter was using to make mud pies. It's just your ordinary old back yard, but suddenly you are filled with happiness, thankfulness, and joy.

That's what my father did. Shining the light of gratitude on his life, he saw what was there that was good.

The great thing about the flashlight of gratitude is that you can use it day or night, no matter where you are or what your circumstances. It works whether we are young or old, fat or thin, rich or poor, sick or well. All we need to do is turn it on.

What it takes to turn it on varies from person to person. There was a renowned surgeon at a week-long workshop who, when asked what surprised or inspired him that week, said, "Nothing." He was invested in being cynical. But something disturbed him; he knew he had "flunked" the test the workshop leader presented— and he was the kind of guy who always ended up at the head of the class. So he began to look around for things to report to the leader. By week's end, he was genuinely engaged in the excitement and wonder of life again. Even the other workshop participants noticed the difference.

$\mathcal{I}$t's All Gratuitous

This is what binds all people and all creation
together—the gratuity of the gift of being.
—MATTHEW FOX

"My only son died five years ago; he was four and a half," writes a contributor to *Slowing Down in a Speeded Up World*. "One of the gifts his death brought was an excuse to stop the rush. For the first year, I allowed grief to wash over me whenever I needed to, and I let myself be open to the healing that surrounds us in this incredible world. I had time for a hug and to talk with my friends; I had vast amounts of time to cherish four and a half years of memories.

"Nowadays it isn't unusual for me to stop in my tracks when a rainbow arches over the bay outside my office window, or a tiny feather drifts down to me from the sky, or a child's laugh at McDonald's brings tears to my eyes.

"I realize how lucky I am, not to have lost my son but to have had him for as long as I did. I'm lucky to have known the importance of certain moments that catch your soul and may never come again."

Gratefulness, or "great fullness" as Brother David

Steindl-Rast calls it, "is the full response of the human heart to the gratuitousness of all that is." He and Matthew Fox remind us that truly every single thing we have has been given to us, not necessarily because we deserve it, but gratuitously, for no known reason, and that the same is true for every living thing. We are connected one to another, to sky and water and tree and snake, by virtue of being here together as part of the wheel of life. Whatever source we believe is the giver—some concept of God or the randomness of the Big Bang—the fact of our incarnation, the fact of the lizard's skin, the rose's scent, the blueness of the sky, is an incredible gift. None of us—bee, flower, person—did anything to earn this gift, nor is anything required of us in return.

When, in a sudden moment—gazing at a field of daffodils, perhaps, or moving luxuriously through warm water, or listening to the painfully beautiful voice of Billie Holiday—we are struck by the truth of this amazingly free "no strings attached" gift, gratitude flows naturally from us, without effort. At such times, we don't need to work at feeling thankful; we just are.

In such transcendent moments, we take our place in the great wheel of life, recognizing our connection to one another and to all of creation. More than that, we actually become part of everything, so that we experience the truth that there is no separation between us and everything else, sound, sight, and feeling.

At such times, gratitude opens our hearts fully and we take in the love, the beauty, the joy that is ours to possess in every moment, in all circumstances. Through the gift of a grateful heart, we merge with the All and remember our rightful home.

A Habit of the Heart

In relation to others, gratitude is good manners;
in relation to ourselves, it is a habit of
the heart and a spiritual discipline.

—DAPHNE ROSE KINGMA

As a young woman in my twenties and thirties, I learned a great deal about thankfulness from Daphne Rose Kingma. We spent a great deal of time together working on books, and again and again I would watch her make a personal connection to the people who came across her path—garbage collectors, long-distance operators, or the person selling coffee on the corner. No matter what was going on in her own life, no matter how rushed or upset she was, she took the time to connect. I'd hear her on the phone with the airline reservations desk. In the course of getting a flight she'd learn the woman's name, where she lived, and the fact that she, like Daphne, loved flashy high heels. Daphne was so genuinely appreciative of the other person's help that the person on the other end of the phone felt washed in a warm bath of love. It was then I realized that while gratitude was a feeling, it could be cultivated. I set out to emulate her (although I still am not as good at it as she).

One of the fascinating things about feelings is that they come and go, like waves in the ocean of our consciousness. Happiness, anger, fear, love, thankfulness—they arise in response to some external or internal trigger and then subside. We feel angry, and then we don't. We are "in love" and then we aren't. We feel thankful, and then it's over. It's particularly easy to see the tide of feelings in a child, where they come and go so quickly and uncensoredly. One minute my daughter is screaming her head off because I have left the room; I return and pick her up—a big smile.

As we grow, one of our spiritual tasks is to move beyond this purely emotional response to life and begin to cultivate positive emotions as "habits of the heart," as Daphne calls them. What this means is that we learn to love even when we don't "feel" loving, be kind when we'd rather be surly, and feel grateful when we don't particularly feel like being thankful. In this way, we turn feelings, which come and go, into conscious attitudes that we act upon even if we don't "feel" like it.

Our attitudes are our mental stances, the positions we hold vis-à-vis life. In some ways, our attitudes determine everything, because they are the glasses through which we see the world. Is the world a wonderful place or a hellhole? All of us know that the answer to that question depends on our attitude on any given day. Has the world changed? Most likely our thinking about it has. When we consciously cultivate positive attitudes, such as love, joy, and gratitude, we begin to "remake" the world. We literally live in a different place because our attitudes about it have changed.

The particular beauty of an attitude of gratitude is that it instantly connects us to everything else. In an important way, it is the recognition of the connection, the switch, between us and the rest of life. And consciously recognizing it opens the flow: the more grateful we are, the more of an abundant sense of life we will experience.

For that's the irony about the relationship between attitudes and feelings. The more you cultivate the attitude, even if you don't feel it, the more you experience the feeling. The more loving we are, the more love we feel. The more joy we radiate, the more comes back our way. And the more thankful we are, the more we experience the richness of spirit that grateful feelings produce.

THE ATTITUDES
OF GRATITUDE

ᴀttitude Is the Only Disability

*We who lived in concentration camps can remember
the men who walked through the huts comforting others,
giving away their last piece of bread. They may have been
few in number, but they offer sufficient proof that
everything can be taken from a man but one thing:
the last of the human freedoms—to choose one's
attitude in any given set of circumstances. . . .*

—Vɪᴄᴛᴏʀ Fʀᴀɴᴋʟ

My friend Annette needs a kidney transplant. Everyone who knows her is amazed at her grateful attitude. Upon hearing the news, rather than adopting a "poor me" stance, she focused on the fact that while waiting for the transplant, she qualifies for a less invasive dialysis method. In telling me about the situation she proclaimed with a radiant face, "I am so thankful. I have four people who have volunteered to be tested to see if they can be a donor. Isn't that great! Four people are willing to give *me* a kidney."

I thought of Annette as I was driving the other day and saw a bumper sticker that proclaimed, "Attitude Is the Only Disability." While I am sure it was a slogan for disabled people's rights, I suddenly realized its larger implications—what we think about our lives, our attitude—has the ability to enable or disable us. As many spiritual teachers have said, we cannot necessarily change our circumstances. But we have complete control over what we think about our circumstances, the meaning we attach to them. No matter our circumstances—even, as Victor Frankl points out, in a situation as horrifying as a concentration camp—we can focus on the positive and make a difference by virtue of our attitude.

Because of her attitude of gratitude, Annette may be "sick," but she is not dis-abled. Through gratitude, she is enhancing her ability to renew and re-create, which comes, as Joan Borysenko puts it, "when we lift ourselves out of the familiar axis and see life from a higher perspective." She is attracting all kinds of people who want to help, everyone from kidney donors and energy healers to coworkers offering to give her their comp time and folks volunteering to cook and clean for her while she's recuperating. We all want to be around her because she is such a teacher of gratitude and joyfulness.

Like no one else, she has proven to me that gratitude is an attitude that can be consciously chosen, no matter what our circumstances. We can focus on the negative and descend into a spiral of negativity and gloom. Or we can choose to look at what's right in any given situation, and become a beacon of love and joy.

Enough Is Enough

The secret to life is to know when enough is enough.

—DR. VINCENT RYAN

This was my father's favorite saying in his final years, and one of the last things he said to me before he died. I was contemplating selling my house and moving to a smaller one, and that was his pronouncement on the subject.

It was kind of ironic, since there he was, a family doctor for forty years, gasping and wheezing over the phone, barely able to speak, dying from smoking too much. But the fact that he learned the lesson late doesn't negate its truth. And it goes straight to the heart of the issue of gratitude: namely, that gratitude makes us feel like we have enough, whereas ingratitude leaves us in a state of deprivation in which we are always looking for something else.

That's why the idea of cultivating "the gratitude attitude" is so popular among twelve-step programs. As Emmet Miller notes in *Gratitude: A Way of Life*, "Gratitude has to do with feeling full, complete, adequate—we have everything we need and deserve; we approach the world with a sense of value." Addictions of all sorts come from a sense of deprivation, a feeling of lack that the user believes can be filled with a substance or activity, whether it's alcohol, drugs, shopping, sex, or food. Caught up in lack, we feed the need but never feel truly satisfied because of course our substance of choice can't fill the lack. Consequently we continue to want more, more, more.

As many people have pointed out, our consumer society owes its very existence to its ability to fuel a sense of never being satisfied. If we were happy about the way we looked, for example, why would we spend billions on cosmetics and plastic surgery? Or on expensive cars that supposedly convey a certain image that we don't have?

An attitude of gratitude gets us off the treadmill and out of the rat race. As we cultivate a true and deep appreciation for what we *do* have, we realize that our sense of lack is, for the most part, an illusion. No matter our material circumstances, the richness of our soul is ultimately what brings us happiness, not another Martini, bigger breasts, or the latest video game. As Lao Tzu proclaimed, "He who knows enough is enough will always have enough."

Always the First Time

Make it new.

—EZRA POUND

I once went to a conference on relationships. Most of the presenters were therapists who had all kinds of elaborate theories about what made good relationships. Then a Buddhist lama got up and said, "I know the secret to keeping love alive. It's simple. All you have to do is act as if you have just met this person and are falling in love. When you meet someone you are interested in, everything they do is wonderful. You love looking at them, hearing what they have to say. Even when they play you country western music, which you hate, you think, 'Well, maybe Tammy Wynette isn't so bad after all.' As time goes on, however, you take the person for granted and fight over Tammy Wynette. So the solution is to see your loved one new again." The therapists were up in arms, proclaiming that such a task was too hard. "Oh," said the lama, "I said it was simple. I didn't say it was easy."

I believe the lama is right. The secret to love—and a sense of joy and gratitude toward all of life—is to see, feel, and hear as if for the First Time. Before the scales of the habitual clouded the brilliant blue sky outside your office window, the tangy juiciness of an orange, or the softness of your loved one's hands. Before you got so used to her kind words, his musical laughter, that they became invisible.

Recently my husband Don had vividly brought home to him the truth of how easy it is to get blinded to the miracles around us. When we first adopted Ana, we couldn't sleep; we were too busy looking into her peaceful face and crying tears of gratitude. Now, a mere four months later, Don, who is home all day with her, finds himself taking her presence for granted, already losing that overwhelming sense of appreciation for her being sent to us. "I get bored," he says, "because it is so much the same, day after day. But her spirit, her presence, is no less a miracle today than it was four months ago, or will be four or forty-years from now. And when I can remember that, I catch myself 'falling asleep' to the miracle, and the awareness wakes me again and my heart once again fills with joy."

When we can live our lives as if it is always the first time—the first time we made love, the first time we gazed upon the face of our beloved, the first time we tasted ice cream, the first time we saw a bird—we won't have to try to experience a sense of gratitude. It will be there, automatically, as a natural response to the beauty and the bounty.

It's OK to Have Good Fortune

There are two ways to live your life. One is as
though nothing is a miracle. The other is as
though everything is a miracle.

—ALBERT EINSTEIN

Recently someone told me that evolutionary biologist Jerod Diamond wrote the current bestselling book, *Guns, Germs, and Steel,* in answer to an aborigine's question, "Why do you guys have all the stuff?" Diamond set out to understand the historical reasons why, but the moral and spiritual issue is what haunts me.

Why *do* we in the West have so much of the stuff? We didn't do anything necessarily to deserve it (and those who think they do deserve it find themselves on a moral slippery slope, which leads to the assumption that those who are suffering from poverty, illness, or plagues did something to deserve *that*). Yes, we may have worked hard to get what we have but at birth, we just woke up in our lives and found ourselves here in easier material circumstances than the vast majority of people in the world. Perhaps one of the reasons so many of us in this culture find it hard to experience an attitude of gratitude is that subconsciously we feel guilty for having so much when others have so little, so we want to ignore the truth of our good fortune.

I remember the first time I realized this personally. I was about twelve and writing an essay for Sunday school. I can't remember the question I was supposed to be answering, but I ended up writing about how lucky I was to be living in the affluent United States instead of on the streets of India.

I don't know about you, but that childish realization now makes me pretty uncomfortable. First, it smacks of cultural imperialism; after all, who am I to say that my life is truly better? Just because we in the West have more stuff doesn't mean we are necessarily happier.

On another level, it makes me feel that I must do something important to continue to deserve my good fortune, and nothing can be important enough. At yet another level, it makes me want to ignore and deny my good fortune so that I don't have to feel guilty.

The issues are complex, and ultimately every person born into relative affluence has to define for themselves what their responsibility is. Here, I simply want to ask the question: Is it possible for us in this culture to truly and fully appreciate what we have been given without feeling guilty? If not, perhaps it is our responsibility to acknowledge our guilt, so that it doesn't block our willingness to be grateful.

ℽou Are Worthy

*You are a child of the universe, no less than the trees
and the stars; you have a right to be here.*

—DESIDERATA

My stepdaughter invited a college friend to our house for a week during winter vacation. I did the usual things hosts do for guests: put out clean sheets and towels, made a bouquet of fresh flowers for the bedside table, found out what she liked and didn't like for meals. I stocked up on bagels and made no food with onions. At dinner, I made polite conversation, inquiring about her interests, her family, her hopes and dreams. At the end of the week, she left, giving no indication of thanks in either word or deed. No note, no present, no phone call.

Now, I didn't entertain her to be thanked, and I wasn't even upset. Rather, I was fascinated about where such a lack of gratitude came from. In talking to my stepdaughter about it, she revealed that she has a hard time with this friend because the young woman has such a low sense of self-esteem. "I spent half my day reassuring her that she looks OK, that she said the right thing, that she is smart and interesting," my stepdaughter complained.

Suddenly I got it—this young woman thinks so

poorly of herself that it doesn't even register that other people find her worthy of flowers and good dinners. What I did was invisible to her because she is invisible to herself!

To experience gratitude, you have to be aware that you've been given something. Whether it's a beautiful head of hair, a trip to Tahiti, or a great new job-because gratitude is the response of the receiver of a gift. It cannot exist if you don't recognize that you have received a gift, and it can't exist if you don't feel worthy of getting the gift. A lack of self-esteem robs you of the joys of gratitude, because you have nowhere to put all that is being given.

By virtue of simply being alive, we receive gifts all the time—if only a new day, a second (or a one-hundredth second) chance—and we are also worthy simply by virtue of being alive. If you have trouble seeing the gifts in your life, perhaps your self-concept needs strengthening.

Take inspiration from Maya Angelou. In a interview with Oprah Winfrey, she was once asked why, despite the hardships she faced, she never doubted herself. Her answer was that she came to realize that God loved her, and from that point on, she no longer had doubts. Because if God loves her, how can she doubt herself?

You are worthy of all that you receive.

Your Soul Has a Purpose

It is up to you to illumine the earth.

—PHILIPPE VENSIER

Tom Chappell, along with his wife, is the owner of Tom's of Maine, the natural personal care products company. In his audiotape *The Soul of Business*, he describes how, despite his incredible material success (a big house, a huge boat, a very successful business), he woke up one day at age forty-three and realized that he felt disconnected from the company and himself. He considered retiring. Then he decided to go to divinity school to become a minister. There he refound his purpose, coming to see that his ministry was to incorporate into the business practices of Tom's of Maine the values that he believed in deeply, and to help other business-people bring soulfulness into their workplaces as well.

If you want the habit of gratitude to grace your life, it is essential that you, like Tom Chappell, develop the belief that you are here on Earth to fulfill some purpose that only you can offer to the world. You are an amazingly rare, totally nonreplicable individual with talents and gifts that the world anxiously needs. The more that you experience the truth of your uniqueness and beauty, the more you will feel gratitude for your particular gifts, and the more you will be able to deliver those gifts.

Unfortunately, not many of us were born to parents who nurtured our individuality, honored our gifts, or helped us recognize our purpose. So as adults we may find it difficult to love ourselves in a wholehearted way that fosters a deep and quiet sense of gratitude for ourselves. In *The Woman's Book of Spirit*, Sue Patton Thoele offers the following meditation:

"It may help to realize the value of gratitude toward ourselves if we were to visualize our heart as a delicate treasure, hand-blown from the rarest ethereal glass. A treasure valuable beyond imagining—fragile, irreplaceable, priceless, and ancient. There is *no* other like it—infinitely precious, existing before time and after infinity.

"In reality, we *were* entrusted with such an inexplicable treasure when we were given the gift of life. . . .

"With your eyes closed, very gently put your hands over your heart and allow your breath to tenderly flow in and out of it. When you feel ready, ask to be given a symbol for your heart. Hold that symbol that you see or sense as carefully as you would a priceless Fabergé egg. Beholding the wonder of your symbol, allow gratitude to flow through you, permeating the very cells of your being. Make a commitment with yourself to cherish and appreciate your heart-self."

The Solution in the Problem

*People are always blaming their circumstances
for what they are. I don't believe in circumstances.
The people who get on in this world are the people
who get up and look for the circumstances they want
and if they can't find them, make them.*

—GEORGE BERNARD SHAW

A therapist I know was treating a woman who'd had a serious stroke and was suffering from aphasia, difficulty in speaking. She didn't seem too troubled by it, but her family considered it a great tragedy. As a young Jewish woman, her verbal ability was a great gift—it had even saved her life. She spoke five languages and survived the Holocaust by becoming a translator for the Nazis in a concentration camp. After the war, she moved to the United States and supported her family teaching foreign languages. Now she struggled for words and her adult children were constantly jumping in to "help" her by filling in her words.

The stroke had changed her in other ways too. Cold and distant as a mother, the stroke had left her very physically affectionate, and she constantly touched her children. However, they were so caught up in the loss of her speaking ability that they didn't recognize that what they were now receiving from her was the kind of affection that they had longed for all their lives.

The therapist taught them that whenever they found themselves frustrated by her lack of verbal acuity, instead of trying to fill in her words, to take a breath and really notice her loving them through her touch. This allowed the woman to have the space she needed to speak, and the children to appreciate the love that was coming from their mother.

The point of this "trick" is to use a source of frustration as a trigger to cultivate an attitude of gratitude. Is there something in your life that you find terribly annoying or difficult? Is there some hidden gift in the annoying situation that you, like the children in this story, can focus on to create an opportunity for gratitude?

For me it's standing in line. I absolutely hate to "waste" time; I live my life at a frenetic pace and don't want anything to get in my way of doing all I have to get done in a day. Until recently, I was the person in the line huffing and rolling my eyes at the wait, jiggling and looking at my watch every few seconds. And when I finally made it to the counter, I was too aggravated from having to wait to be pleasant to the person on the other side of the counter. But since life is full of lines, I finally decided to change my approach. Instead of being annoyed, I decided to see waiting in line as a wonderful opportunity to slow down, to take a few conscious breaths, become aware of my body, and release as much muscle tension as I could. The waits are as long as ever—but now I am grateful for the chance to stop.

The Time Is Now

*We can spend a whole lifetime enjoying
various benefits and not appreciate their value until we
are deprived of them. How many lovers boldly contemplate
separation, fondly imagining that they have had enough
of the beloved. And yet as soon as they actually experience
separation, they burn up with longing.*

—JAMI

Boy, do I recognize myself in Sufi Jami's quote! Retroactive gratitude I call it—realizing after something is over or someone is gone that I really appreciated what I had, but wasn't aware of it until it was gone. Good health, the smile of a loved one, a job that allowed for creativity and self-expression—the list of what we might have taken for granted is endless.

Failing to appreciate what we had until it's "too late" leads to regret, one of the most insidious negative feelings there is. Regret is a poison that keeps us in the past: If only I had told him more often I was thankful for all he gave me, maybe he would not have left me; if only I had been more appreciative of my legs before I got hit by the car; if only I had told her how much her kind words meant to me... if only, if only. Our minds spin around, creating story upon story of how life could have been better if we had taken less for granted.

Whenever I find myself swirling around in a fog of retroactive gratitude, I do two things. First, I take time to consciously thank the person or thing I have belatedly discovered my gratitude for. If the person is alive, I thank them via letter or phone call. If not, I send a mental thanks, as I do for a situation I am grateful for. Second, I take a hard look at my current life, at the things I might be taking for granted right now.

While we can never know if being grateful in the moment would have created a different outcome— maybe he wouldn't have left if you had nagged less and been more grateful, but then again, maybe not—what is for sure is that the more we give thanks *now* for what we do have, the fewer regrets we will have in the future, no matter what happens. Maybe you can't tell your sister who just died how grateful you were for her presence in your life, but right now you can tell your husband, your child, and your best friend what they mean to you.

Let the fact of our regret send us into the world with ever more appreciation for the gifts we have been given, and a commitment to communicate that appreciation as often as possible.

The Joy of Living

*It was then I learned that gratitude is the best feeling
I would ever have, the ultimate joy of living. It was better
than sex, better than winning the lottery, better than
watching your daughter graduate from college, better and
deeper than any other feeling; it is perhaps the genesis of
all other really good feelings in the human repertoire.*

—LEWIS SMEDES, AFTER ALMOST DYING

In *A Pretty Good Person,* Lewis Smedes, a professor of
theology and ethics at Fuller Theological Seminary,
tells the story of collapsing in his Minnesota apartment
on a "frightfully cold December morning. . . .

"My lungs it turned out, had been spattered by a
buckshot of blood clots; and for a couple of days at the
hospital I tilted in death's direction. On the fourth day a
benign Norwegian physician by the name of Hans
Engman leaned over my bed and congratulated me on
surviving the twenty-to-one odds that medical statistics
had stacked up against me. . . .

"A couple of nights later—in the moody hush that
settles on a hospital room at two o'clock in the morning,
alone, with no drugs in me to set me up for it—I was

seized with a frenzy of gratitude.... I blessed the Lord above for the almost unbearable goodness of being alive on this good earth in this good body at this present time."

In doing research for this book, it was amazing to me how many people related a similar story—that it took a brush with death to awaken them to a sense of gratitude. I read about how car accidents, cancer experiences, boating mishaps, and other life-threatening difficulties were wake-up calls to live with more thankfulness for the ordinary things of life. These weren't intellectual decisions; rather, each person was overwhelmed with a tremendous feeling of gratitude, as Lewis Smedes describes, and from that feeling made a pledge to cultivate gratefulness on a daily basis.

My question is this: Do *you* need to almost die to experience the joy available in this moment? Or is it possible, right now, to tap into the amazingly wonderful fact that you are alive, breathing in and breathing out, able to take in the world through your senses, able to smile to a stranger, caress a loved one, touch the soft down of a baby's cheek? We do not need to almost die to feel the wonderful warm bath of gratitude. In any moment, we can experience the world as new again, and touch the joyful ecstasy those who have gone through near-death experiences relate.

Think for a moment of something you almost lost but didn't—a friend in an argument, your car that was stolen but then abandoned, a breast, your life. Does your heart naturally swell in thanksgiving for their continued presence in your life?

An Ever-Increasing Spiral

*As I express my gratitude, I become more deeply
aware of it. And the greater my awareness, the greater
my need to express it. What happens here is a spiraling
ascent, a process of growth in ever expanding
circles around a steady center.*

—BROTHER DAVID STEINDL-RAST

"My Russian grandmother was my greatest teacher
in gratitude," a coworker recently told me. "We
were very poor and I often would complain about not
having this or that. Any time we went anywhere, she
would use whatever happened as a lesson in giving
thanks. We'd walk down the streets of New York and
see a man without legs begging for food, and she would
say, 'Now you send up a prayer right now to God
thanking him for your legs and for the food in your
belly.' She wouldn't do it to feel superior to the man or
to make me feel guilty, but to teach me that around us
every day are ways to remind ourselves of the bounty
we have, no matter what our circumstances, and the
more we give thanks, the more likely it is that the blessings will continue. For years in my adolescence, I

rejected her teaching. But lately I've begun to notice that the more I give thanks, the better my life goes. When I become ungrateful, things tend to fall apart."

A lot of the recent writing on gratitude makes it sound like some kind of insurance policy, as if the reason to feel grateful is to make sure that good things will continue to come our way. That feels spiritually materialistic to me, like praying for a pink Cadillac or a mink stole. True gratitude is a natural response to the miracle of life as we experience it moment to moment, a sense of abundance from the heart that is independent of our desires for the future.

That said, it does seem to be true that whatever we focus on tends to increase. Have you ever noticed that if you learn a new word you suddenly hear it everywhere? Or your friend introduces you to blue lobelia and you suddenly notice it blooming all over?

Exactly why this happens is something of a mystery, but I believe it's because everything is around us *all the time*. We are choosing, mostly unconsciously, to notice certain things and not others because we just cannot pay attention to everything. As we change what we pay attention to, we notice *that* more. Scientists have proposed that something more amazing is at work—that reality is open to the mind's causal influence and is, in the words of David L. Cooperider, "often profoundly created through our anticipatory images, values, plans, intentions, beliefs and the like." This suggests that we actually participate in creating what happens to us by the power of our positive or negative imagery.

In either case, the more we are grateful, the more we will have to be grateful for. Even if nothing more or better happens, our eyes are opened to the gifts that were always there. As Susan Jeffers notes, "When we focus on abundance, our life feels abundant; when we focus on lack, our life feels lacking. It is purely a matter of focus."

95

Start Where You Are

If you haven't got all the things you want,
be grateful for the things you don't have
that you don't want.

—ANONYMOUS

Sometimes we are in such a negative state that the only way we can connect to a sense of gratefulness is to count all the bad things that aren't happening to us: well, the dog didn't get hit by a car today; I don't have Alzheimer's yet; my kid didn't pierce her nose today; an earthquake didn't strike.

Counting blessings that are blessings by virtue of their not having struck, the more outrageous the better, is a great mood-elevator. By the time you recite your list to a loved one or friend, you should be feeling a whole lot better.

But there is a serious aspect to this as well. When you really think about it, *isn't* it wonderful that the tornado didn't strike? Isn't it *great* that the house didn't burn down? (It's a real possibility. Three of my closest friends have had their homes or businesses burn to the ground.) Sometimes we need to look at what hasn't befallen us to wake ourselves up to the joys of our ordinary life.

Often we arrive at this place by hearing about the misfortunes of others; "Oh, thank God it wasn't my child in that car crash"; "I'm so grateful that it's not my husband who's losing his job"; "Think of all those poor people who lost their homes." Such reactions are human nature, I suppose, and yet it would be wonderful if we didn't need the sorrows of other people to remind us of the blessings in our own lives. Rather, if we consciously count our blessings on a daily basis, including those that are blessings by virtue of their not happening, instead of experiencing a sense of grateful relief when we hear about someone else's misfortune perhaps we will be spurred into the action that comes from an awakened sense of compassion.

THE PRACTICES OF GRATITUDE

Beginning to tune into even the minutest
feelings of . . . gratitude softens us. . . .
If we begin to acknowledge these moments
and cherish them . . . then no matter how
fleeting and tiny this good heart may
seem, it will gradually, at its own speed,
expand.

—PEMA CHÖDRÖN

OW WE COME TO THE NEXT stage of our journey, which is where we begin to put our attitudes into action. Here we don't just *feel* grateful, but we move to express our feelings of gratefulness in a variety of ways that enrich our lives and the lives of those around us. This is where we truly ripen as souls, for it is easy to pay lip service to the idea of gratitude and not take the final step of *embodying* it. But when we begin to practice gratitude, we create a powerful resonance between our thoughts and our actions, and our souls shine forth in all their brillance.

Exercise Daily

Your future depends on many things, but mostly on you.
——FRANK TYGER

Even though I have spent the last twenty-five years as an editor and a writer, I am continually amazed that writing is a muscle that must be exercised. When I or my authors do it every day, it comes relatively easily, just like running a mile does for a marathoner. When too much time has passed since I last sat down in front of the computer, my brain is creaky like an athlete coming back after an injury. Once, when I had not written for a month, I despaired that I could ever do it again.

The same is true for fostering any attitude. The more you do it, the easier it is to do. In fact, I'm convinced that this is the difference between an optimist and a pessimist. A pessimist is someone who has exercised the muscles of negativity and lack till they are strongly habitual, while an optimist is a person who has developed thankfulness and a can-do attitude until these are second nature. We all have the choice of which muscles we want to strengthen. With practice, we can become joy-filled participants in the game of life, thankful to do our part and relishing in the sheer pleasure of play.

THE PRACTICES
OF GRATITUDE

When I think of someone who really exercises her gratitude muscles, I think of Peris. She's the kind of person who calls her friends out of the blue to thank them for being in her life. She comes from a large Croatian family, replete with all kinds of screwball uncles and zany aunts, the kind of family many of us would run from. Listening to her stories, you begin to appreciate your own quirky family members in the same way she does. Recently I called her to ask her about gratitude. She didn't get back to me right away, and when she finally did, she said my call had reminded her that she hadn't been feeling very thankful lately and was grateful for the wake-up.

Like Peris, you have to practice or the muscle will wither. Developing the muscle of gratitude is just like exercising any other. At first it will seem weird, awkward, perhaps even hard to do. But if you keep at it every day, soon you won't even have to think about it.

Whether you keep a gratitude journal or start a practice of thinking about all you are grateful for as you drive to or from work, creating some daily ritual really helps build the muscle. Only you know what will work best for you—a file on your computer, a beautiful blank book, an audiotape in your car. Whichever format you pick, make a commitment to list ten things every day that you are grateful for. Pretty soon it will be second nature. Here's the beginning of my list: "I didn't get in a car accident; my computer worked; my baby is healthy; it stopped raining; I had steak for dinner; my house is warm and dry; my sister called...."

THE PRACTICES
OF GRATITUDE

Chose Gratefulness "In Spite Of"

As you wander on through life, sister/brother,
whatever be your goal, keep your eye
upon the donut, and not upon the hole.
—Sign in the Mayflower Coffee Shop, Chicago

Bestselling author Iyanla Venzant, who penned such inspirational books as *Acts of Faith* and *One Day My Soul Just Opened,* has lived the prototypical rags-to-riches story. A former welfare recipient, she was about forty when her life began to turn around. Through it all, she claims, her sense of gratitude kept her going. "I'm grateful for everything," she says, "from being homeless to sitting in a half-million-dollar house."

This remarkable woman is pointing to something very important about gratitude—that we can experience it even "in spite of" something else: that our friend is lying in a hospital dying, that millions of people are starving as you read this book, that our own lives have trials and tribulations that might be sorely testing us.

We can't wait until everything is OK—with us or with the rest of the world—to feel thankful, or we will never experience it at all. "The world is too bent for unshadowed joy," Lewis Smedes points out, and so we

THE PRACTICES
OF GRATITUDE

must catch and kiss our joy as it flies by, even in the midst of sorrow or suffering. This is not to imply that we deny suffering, but just that we not allow our suffering to blind us to the beauty and joy that surrounds us no matter what else is going on.

It's a matter of where you choose to put your attention. Try the following experiments: Pick one morning and stop every hour on the hour and notice what went wrong in that time period. The traffic was terrible and you were late to work; the weather was gloomy and cold; your boss complained about the project you've worked so hard on. That afternoon, stop every hour on the hour and notice what went right: An old friend called out of the blue; the sun came out; you did an excellent job on the sales letter.

Did you feel more alive in the morning or in the afternoon?

Revel in the Ordinary

Normal day, let me be aware of the treasure you are.
Let me learn from you, love you, bless you before you
depart. Let me not pass you by in quest of some rare and
perfect tomorrow. Let me hold you while I may, for it may
not always be so. One day I shall dig my nails into the
earth, or bury my face in the pillow, or stretch myself
taut, or raise my hands to the sky and want, more
than all the world, your return.

—MARY JEAN IRON

It's hard to appreciate the ordinary, except in contrast to something hard or challenging. I am always reminded of the truth of this when I've been sick. When I am well, I take my physical being for granted. I don't particularly notice how I feel; I'm simply not aware of it. But when I've been sick and begin to feel better, I am filled with immense gratitude for how good it feels *not* to be sick—not to have an aching head, a burning throat, leaden muscles and joints. I feel exactly as I normally do, but *now I notice how great that is.*

Other people experience this sensation from a close call in a car or plane, an almost-bankruptcy, anything that shakes us out of complacency and wakes us to the wonder of our ordinary existence.

The trick, of course, is to learn how to have that awareness without having to be sick, almost lose your house, or get hurt in a car crash. One way to do it is to pick an ordinary task, something you do every day, and decide that just for today, you will do it with awareness. It can be anything—washing dishes, chopping vegetables, making the bed. Instead of doing it while thinking about something else, such as the dinner that still needs to be made or how mad you are at the driver who cut you off, you actually pay attention to the task itself rather than being on automatic pilot. Notice the high-pitched whirring of the vacuum cleaner, the hard-yet-soft feel of the ribbed hose in your hand, the sight of the white dog hairs against the hardwood floor as they are sucked into the vacuum....

This kind of awareness practice, the more specific the better, is great for fostering a sense of appreciation for the ordinary. As Rick Field notes, "When we pay attention, whatever we are doing—whether it be cooking, cleaning or making love—is transformed.... We begin to notice details and textures that we never noticed before; everyday life becomes clearer, sharper, and at the same time more spacious." Our eyes are opened once again to the miracles of the absolutely ordinary and joy fills our hearts.

What Do You Really Need?

The grand essentials to happiness in this life are something
to do, something to love, and something to hope for.
—JOSEPH ADDISON

A friend of mine who has health problems recently decided to sell her big, beautiful house in the country and move to a small condo in the city. It is easier for her to manage the day-to-day basics of life in a smaller home, close to public transportation, and the financial pressure is much lighter. But she's been finding it quite difficult to let go of all the beautiful attributes of her big house, particularly since she's discovered that her budget won't allow for certain amenities she was counting on. "Yesterday," she confided to me, "I found out that I can't have the French doors I had my heart set on. They're just too expensive. I started to feel terrible, but then I asked myself, honestly, do you *need* French doors? The answer of course was No, and I felt much better."

When we focus on what we truly need, as opposed to what we might like or want, life gets much simpler, and it's much easier to feel grateful. Because, when it comes right down to it, there's not a whole lot that we really need. Do we *need* a cherry-red Jeep? A trip to

Barbados? What about a television? A garden? Time off with family? A job that gives you a sense of purpose?

It's helpful to look around and figure out what you need to be happy. If you really think about it, it's not a long list: food, shelter, rest, loved ones, something meaningful to do. That's about it. All the rest of the stuff of life are wants. Important wants, but wants nonetheless. For example, at the top of my "need" list is a hot tub. I go in at least once a day, often twice, and it helps my back and my temperament a lot. But I lived for years without one and got along just fine, so on reflection I would have to say that it's not a true need.

My friend's remark about the French doors has been incredibly helpful in cultivating an attitude of gratitude. Now, every time I get caught up in wanting something and bemoaning the fact that I can't have it, I ask myself, "But do I *need* this to be happy?" It's amazing how often the answer is No. Give it a try yourself right now.

Do the Work of Forgiveness

*There are many ways to victimize people. One way is
to convince them that they are victims.*

—KAREN HWANG

Nothing blocks feelings of gratitude more than
anger and resentment. That's why the practice of
gratitude requires the work of forgiveness. We can't feel
grateful to our parents for what we received from them
when we are still angry about their abuse, self-
involvement, insensitivity, alcoholism, or neglect. Nor
can we receive the gifts of a relationship that has ended
when we still feel hurt over betrayal, angry over deceit,
sorrowful over abandonment.

Nor should we. Trying to force ourselves to feel
grateful when such strong negative feelings exist only
compounds the injury. We have been hurt. Let's not
deny our woundedness on top of everything else.
Healing, in the form of acknowledging the grievance
and grieving the loss or wound, needs to happen first.

However, there comes a time in the process of emotional resolution for forgiveness. For only forgiveness
can move us out of the victim stance and free us to move
on. Depending on the kind of wound you have suffered,

this may be deep psychological and spiritual work. No one can talk you into it. No one can do it for you. Only you can come to the place where you want to forgive.

What helps the forgiveness process is to understand that resentment is a second-hand emotion, a cover for underlying feelings that have never been expressed. That's why it is useful to do a practice called "A Damage Report." In a letter (that you never send) to your abuser, write down all the effects the wounding had on you, in as much detail as you possibly can. Don't hold back. Then create a boundary, something like: I will get up and leave the room if someone is verbally abusing me; or, I will not stay with anyone who is abusing drugs. This will help you develop trust that you will protect yourself against such circumstances and people in the future. Then write a note of forgiveness to yourself for not having stated your boundary before, and a note of thanks to the other person for the learning, so that it won't happen again.

If you really take the time to express fully your needs and pain and state your new boundary, chances are you'll begin to be grateful for the lessons the wounding has taught you, whether it's to stand up for yourself, to be kinder toward others, to stop drinking, whatever. At some point you realize that you are a better, stronger, more loving person than you might have been if you hadn't been so hurt, and you recognize the gift in your particular suffering. In that moment, you move from victim to victor, from victor to venerated teacher.

Forgiveness leads to gratitude, and not just gratitude in general but, in a beautifully healing movement, to an outpouring of appreciation for the very things that caused such pain in the first place. Thus is our suffering redeemed.

℘ractice Wonderment

Oh, for the wonder that
bubbles into my soul.

—D. H. LAWRENCE

Recently I took my one-year-old daughter to the zoo for the first time. Her eyes almost popped out of her head when she saw an elephant. And when I gave her her first scoop of ice cream, her joy knew no bounds. Her little body wriggled, her eyes sparkled, and she brought out the biggest smile. The truth is elephants *are* amazing creatures, and ice cream *is* just as delicious the one-thousandth time as the first. But we adults have lost our wonderment, and so we can't appreciate elephants and ice cream as much.

In wonderment, children are our greatest teachers. Wonder is a natural state, one that we often lose track of as we become numb to life. Since wonderment is the willingness to be surprised by life, and gratitude springs from wonderment, to practice gratefulness we need to let life surprise us, with a glorious sunset, a luxurious back rub, a mysterious phone call, or the kindness of a stranger. The problem with adulthood is that we become jaded: Oh yes, another great sunset, another fabulous dinner, another birthday present.

We can recapture our sense of wonderment at any moment. All it takes is to open our senses and let the world come into us anew. Try it for one minute. First, listen to the sounds around you: perhaps an airplane is overhead. Isn't it amazing that airplanes can fly? It doesn't seem possible. What kinds of scents are in the air? I can smell jasmine. Isn't it amazing that so many flowers have such distinctive scents?

Now turn to your sense of sight. Really notice what's around you: the grain in the wooden door; the black letters against the white page, the bright yellow bananas in the bowl. Isn't it amazing that you can see? Isn't it fascinating to wonder if everyone can see yellow the same way as you? Isn't it marvelous that you can have a banana even though they grow thousands of miles away?

We can touch wonder in every moment as we slow down and perceive the world around us as if for the first time. And when we contact wonder, we know thankfulness for the most ordinary, extraordinary things of life.

Don't Compare

Life begets life. Energy creates energy.
It is by spending oneself that one becomes rich.

—SARAH BERNHARDT

Driving home the other day, I heard on the radio that as the stock market went up, so did the salaries of corporate bosses who take stock options as part of their compensation. Last year, the head of Disney made $10 million, another guy in L.A. made $45 million, and that's not even considering Bill Gates. I could feel my blood turning green with envy, and all sense of gratitude for my own life—that I have a wonderful, loving family, close friends, a beautiful house, fundamentally good health—went flying out the window. "If only I could have just *one* of their many millions," I thought, "then my life would be happy."

The truth is, of course, that happiness is an inside job and, beyond the subsistence level, money truly has very little to do with our happiness. But most of us are convinced that money can indeed buy happiness. The universality of that feeling struck me a few years ago when I read about a study that asked people how much money they thought they needed to be happy.

Everyone, no matter what they made, thought they needed more. People who made $20,000 thought $30,000 would do it; folks at $45,000 were convinced $65,000 was the magic number, people at $100,000 were sure $200,000 was it. The only thing that changed was that as people's incomes grew, their magic number grew exponentially (proving like nothing else that the "gimme hole" only grows through feeding). I realized then that there is something in human nature—well, at least in contemporary Western human nature—that will always long for more and envy those who have it, and the only way to deal with that trait is to acknowledge it: Oh, there you are again, and then turn our attention back to what matters.

Here's a practice for dealing with envy. Spend one day with one pocket of change and one empty pocket. Each time you find yourself envious of someone, put a coin in the empty pocket and ask yourself, "What is there that I am noticing in the other person that I want to find in myself?" (Because you wouldn't notice it if it weren't already in you.) If it's money, is it the freedom? The chance to play that money buys? A sense of security? Whatever it is—more play, a sense of security, free time—you can work on getting more of it in your life, no matter the circumstances.

I can choose to spend my time envying Bill Gates, the housewife who doesn't have to work because her wealthy lawyer husband provides for all her needs, and the person down the street who just inherited a large estate from his mother, or I can begin to understand what I am really longing for in myself.

I use envy as a trigger to remembering that I want to do a better job of giving myself away, as Sarah Bernhardt counsels, so that I will experience a true sense of richness no matter what my material resources. I can't keep the green-eyed monster from rearing its ugly head from time to time, but I can use its appearance to rededicate myself to using myself fully on behalf of the world as a whole. The feeling of abundance—great fullness—that doing the work our soul is here to do is better than any old million dollars.

119

Transform Expectations into No Matter Whats

It seems to me that we often, almost sulkily,
reject the good that God offers us because,
at the moment, we expected some other good.

—C. S. Lewis

The most ungrateful person I know is an older woman who can't see the beauty of her life because she is so bitter that it didn't turn out the way she thought it should. She has a lovely home and garden, healthy, bright, successful children, a fifty-year marriage, and the means and health to travel. No one in her immediate family has died or been seriously ill; she's never known poverty or lack; she is, from all external measures, highly privileged, with much to be grateful for. And yet all of what she has is completely invisible to her because it somehow doesn't match the picture of what she expected. Her kids don't live close enough or visit often enough; she wishes there was even more money; her marriage isn't as loving as she desires. Her ingratitude is a self-fulfilling prophecy, for the more she complains, the more lonely and isolated she finds herself as friends and family grow weary of her moaning.

To me, this acquaintance is an important teacher in the practice of gratitude—a vivid example of how expectations can create blinders so that we can't even see the true blessings of our lives. Expectations are the killers of gratitude and joy: If you expect to live in the Taj Mahal, your cozy little cottage will feel pretty awful; if you expect your son to become a doctor, you can't appreciate him for the fine bodyworker that he is; if you focus on how you are going to be miserable without a BMW, your trusty, rusty Toyota that reliably gets you around will only bring you misery.

Having hopes, dreams, and visions for the future are one thing; it's important to have goals and schemes pulling us into the future. But we need to be careful that such envisioning doesn't get in the way of appreciating the things we have in the here and now. Let's not miss the beauty of our actual lives while we're lusting after a mythical perfect life.

If we expect someone or something outside ourselves to make us happy, we lose our power. The truth is we can't count on anything except our ability to choose how to respond to what happens to us. One way to counteract the tendency to look outside ourselves for happiness is to practice No Matter What. Before you go into a situation, ask yourself, "What is it that I can learn, accomplish, or experience here, no matter what happens?" Let's say you have to give a speech and are nervous about how it will be received. Your No Matter What might be, "No matter what, I want to experience a sense of peace while talking. As I look out into the audience, I'll remember to breathe and notice that at my core there is peace." Afterwards, no matter what else happened—that people appeared bored, or no one came up to thank you—you can still appreciate yourself for having kept your commitment to experience peacefulness.

When we practice No Matter What, we are no longer hooked by expectations to externals—other people, other events—but are free to choose what we will focus on to make us happy.

123

Develop a Good Memory

Gratitude is the memory of the heart; therefore forget
not to say often, I have all I ever enjoyed.

—LYDIA CHILD

Sometimes life is so challenging, so painful, that it is
plain impossible to feel grateful for anything that is
going on. At such moments, it's nice to have a reservoir
of contentment to fall back on, a storehouse of joyful
memories to open and hold onto as you navigate
through the dark night of the soul.

A good memory doesn't just work for really tough
times. It also helps to smooth over the little bumps and
glitches of ordinary life, particularly in relationships.
When I find myself annoyed with something my husband is saying, for instance, if I can remember the piece
of angel food cake he brought me as a surprise yesterday
while I was working, my annoyance melts as my gratitude is engaged. A good memory also helps, for example, when you find yourself angry at a coworker for
failing to meet a deadline. Recalling with gratitude how
often she has come through for you in the past, graciously let her off the hook.

A good memory keeps us from losing our perspective, from being so caught up in the work of the here and now that we forget the larger bounty of our lives. I'm not suggesting that we should deny our suffering or ignore the problems in our lives, just that we can balance them with joy and peacefulness by remembering moments, events, and people that we are grateful for.

What are the things in your life that, looking back, you are most thankful for? Notice what comes up without your reaching for it. This practice is not about making a laundry list but of allowing yourself to notice what really sticks with you. These are your Highlights of Happiness: the birth of your son; recovery from a serious illness, a certain way the light falls in your bedroom—whatever they are, they are *your* precious moments to be taken out and savored any time you need them.

Take Time to Smell the Roses

*It's good to have an end to journey toward; but it's
the journey that matters, in the end.*

—URSULA K. LEGUIN

The practice of gratitude requires that you slow down long enough to notice what is right in front of your nose. If you are speeding through the day, chances are you are overlooking the blessings that are all around you. No matter what our circumstances, we can slow down enough to notice and give thanks to our breath going in and out, the food we are about to eat, the book we are reading, the kindness of the stranger we bumped into. As we take the time to open our five senses to the world around us, we won't miss the shooting star, the life-altering words, the tiny blue violets. And our lives will be enriched by the bounty all around us.

We've all been told to stop and smell the roses a million times, we forget it as promptly as we hear it. So what will actually get us to do it?

The trick is to use the goings-on in daily life as triggers. In his book *Stopping*, David Kundtz suggests the practice of Stillpoints, stops for a very brief time, that are made in the "unfilled moments in life": while waiting for the microwave to heat your coffee, standing in line, walking from one appointment to the next, sitting at a red light. Sitting or standing, you "stop, breathe, and remember." Stop, notice a breath in and a breath out, and remember. The remembering can be any message that is powerful and important for you: that you are loved, that you are filled with peace and joy, that you have plenty of time to do what you have to, that you can notice the world around you in this moment. If you are trying to increase your sense of gratitude, perhaps your message can be something like, "I notice the gifts surrounding me in this moment."

David suggests that you do Stillpoints many times a day in order to increase your sense of inner peace and awareness. What trigger would work best for you? What will work best is something that causes you to pause anyway, and that you experience several times a day, like a red light or a bathroom break. For the monks and nuns at Plum Village in France, it is the telephone. They notice three breaths before they answer the phone. It doesn't matter what you choose, only that you begin to practice.

Attitudes of gratitude

Focus on What's Right

Thank God for what doesn't need healing.

—JOAN BORYSENKO

We are so incredibly well trained to notice what's wrong in any given relationship, work situation, or experience that it's easy to overlook what's right. That's not surprising, because our entire education system trains us to notice flaws and mistakes: in school, the wrong answers are marked, not the right ones. In relationships, we spend a lot of time, energy, and money, often with the help of therapists, working on fixing what's wrong. At work, we study our failures and mistakes for hidden clues so that we can prevent them from happening again.

But what if we have it backward? What would we be like now if all the answers we got correct on every test had been marked? What if we spent as much energy in relationships noticing and appreciating the other person's gifts and talents and the strengths and beauty of the relationship itself as we do exposing and dealing with its flaws? What if, at work, we spent an equal amount of time looking at what is working and how we can do more of that as we do analyzing what's wrong?

An "asset focus"—noticing and appreciating, as Joan Borysenko puts it, what *doesn't* need healing, is an incredibly powerful tool for creating connection, fostering creative thinking, and overcoming obstacles. I saw this most powerfully at an office retreat in which we honored the twelve people who worked at Conari Press. We went around the room, focusing on one person at a time. The rules were simple: Anyone who wished to could say what they appreciated about that person; no one had to speak; no one could interrupt or interject; and the receiver had to just listen without comment.

We had allotted an hour for the practice; it ended up taking three, because there was so much we wanted to say about each person. People laughed and cried. By the end, the sense of camaraderie, connection, and team were the strongest I ever felt. The next day, we came up with some of the best book ideas we've ever thought of. I still remember vividly what people said.

You can do this with any group—work team, church group, in your own family. I really encourage you to try it. It's one of the most magical things I've ever done.

Be Willing to Embrace What Shows Up

I have learned, in whatsoever state I am in,
therewith to be content.

—Saint Paul

I once studied with a group that believed life is an active force at work on an individual. They believed that for every person, there are three circles of influence: you, other people, and life itself. All three are interconnected and interpenetrating: just as you influence and are influenced by those around you, so does life influence and is influenced by you. (Many people believe that God operates in a similar way.)

I found the idea quite reassuring. Instead of feeling alone in an uncaring, random universe that threw trouble my way willy-nilly, I could take comfort in feeling that there was some two-way relationship between life and me. Which might also mean that there was a good reason that certain things showed up and not others. This made it easier for me to be content with what happens in my life, rather than always yearning for something else.

Such contentment is important to cultivate, because

life has a way of throwing us curves: We want a Persian cat, but a stray lands at our doorstep; we want to have a baby but are plagued by infertility; we want that fabulous new job, but are passed over; we want to be married to the man of our dreams, but get involved in a series of short relationships instead. Unless we embrace what shows up in our lives, we will never get the benefits of the lessons life is trying to teach us: We'll never love the mutt, adopt a baby, be available for the even better job, or learn the skills that a long-term relationship requires.

It is only by being grateful for what is that we experience contentment, and it is contentment with what is that makes us happy in the moment—and available to whatever else life has in store for us.

Try the following practice for a week. In the course of your daily life, whenever you encounter something that is not your idea of a good thing, ask yourself, "If everything that is happening is right, how is this right?" What's *right* about the fight with your mother, the fender-bender, your aching back? Without negating what's wrong, ask yourself what function or need is the event serving? Maybe what's right about the fight is that you are learning to say No; maybe the fender bender is a wake-up call that you are too stressed out; maybe your aching back is a reminder that your body wants some exercise. Again, this is not to deny, suppress, or ignore the difficulty or pain you might be experiencing, but rather to take the meaning from the suffering so that the lesson won't have to be learned again. At the end of the week, reflect on the experience. What changed in you as a consequence of looking for what's right?

133

ℒook for the Hidden Blessings of Difficult Situations

Some people once brought a blind man to Jesus and asked him, 'Rabbi, who sinned, this man or his parents, that he was born blind?' They all wanted to know why this terrible curse had fallen on this man. And Jesus answered, 'It was not that this man sinned, or his parents, but that the words of God might be manifest in him.' He told them not to look for why the suffering came but to listen for what the suffering could teach them.

—WAYNE MULLER

Gratitude is an all-out experience. It's cheating to be grateful only for the good things that happen and to shun the bad. This isn't to say that we *want* bad things to happen to us, just that if we can be grateful for the soul-lessons inherent in the difficulties that befall us, then our souls will be able to grow and mature. Otherwise, we never progress, because we fail to use the hardships that dog us to become more loving, more patient, more present, more kind.

The people whom I admire most in the world say without reservation that the hardest things they had to

THE PRACTICES
OF GRATITUDE

face, cancer, the death of a child, a bankruptcy, or job loss, had been their greatest teachers and that they were grateful for the lessons. For me it has been dealing with chronic pain.

When I was a senior in college I hurt my back. It was the first time my body ever betrayed me. Until then, I always considered it just a handy container to take my mind where it wanted to go. But suddenly I couldn't move, and I had to pay attention to it. Eventually I spent over a year in bed.

It's been twenty years since then, and my back continues to be one of my greatest teachers. I've learned a lot about patience (a hard lesson for me!) and impermanence (just because it hurts like hell today doesn't mean it will tomorrow). I've learned the value of physical discipline ("No time to do those boring back exercises?" my body says. "I'll show you!"). I've learned that I can't push myself beyond limits that often I still don't recognize until after I've exceeded them. That even doing everything "right" is no guarantee I'll be free from pain. I've learned to let go of my wanting it to be better, and I've learned about how much I still exist even if I am able to do absolutely nothing. Now, in theory, I could have learned these things some other way, and perhaps I might have. But the truth of my life is that I have learned them through chronic pain—and I am grateful for the lessons, if not for the pain.

Right now, write down the ten hardest or most terrible things that ever happened to you. As you look over the list, can you see the gifts that each of them brought?

Metaphysical teacher Daniel T. Peralta suggests that when you are suffering from some difficulty whose blessing is invisible to you, you say the following prayer: "I am willing to see the gift in this experience. May the lessons be revealed to me, and may I become stronger and clearer."

137

Teach Gratitude to Your Young Ones

Celebrate what you want to see more of.

—Tom Peters

Many of us in the baby-boom generation, once we were grown, rebelled against "Emily Post, pinky-in-the-air"-type manners. Because we rejected the phony, pro forma "Now what do you say to Mrs. So-and-So?" style of gratitude, lots of us neglected to teach our children how connect to a true sense of gratefulness. As a result, the younger generations seem to have an overinflated sense of entitlement that blocks any sense of gratitude.

I think our neglect of this important aspect of spiritual guidance also comes from having been "shoulded" so much in *our* childhoods. How many of us were told we should eat our peas because "children were starving in China (or Armenia or India)"? How many of us were told we should be grateful because we had a bicycle and running shoes and a lovely bedroom and so many other kids around the world have nothing except bare dirt? As I mentioned before, such remarks only serve to make us feel guilty, and guilt just makes us want to avoid whatever is provoking it.

As recipients of such training, we already know a lot about what doesn't help foster an attitude of gratitude in children. But what does work? Not surprisingly, the same things that work for adults—teaching our kids an asset focus and a conscious counting of their blessings without a guilt trip.

When you're helping your children with homework, if they are having trouble with something break the task into parts and ask them to figure out what part they already know how to do. "OK, you have to write a report on Native American life in New Mexico. You're great at knowing where to look for information, and you're also good at describing out loud what you've read. Maybe you can read the book, then talk out loud to me and we'll tape it. You can then transcribe it and you'll have your report." By reminding them of what they are good at, they will begin to focus on their strengths, and can begin to figure out how to use those resources on their own behalf.

Then, each night, I suggest you do the following bedtime ritual. As you put your children to bed, spend at least three minutes of private time, after books and bathroom and teeth-brushing, and ask them to tell you one thing they did that they appreciate themselves for and one thing someone else did that they are thankful for. You can remind them of the things they learned about themselves while doing homework if they are having trouble thinking of something to appreciate in themselves. If you're not there, ask your spouse or the babysitter to perform this ritual with your children. The more you help your children focus on what they appreciate about themselves and those around them, the more they will overflow with optimism, hopefulness, and joy.

THE PRACTICES
OF GRATITUDE

Dedicate This Moment

It is better to give and receive.

—ACTS 20:35

O ne of the wonderful effects of a sense of gratitude is the desire to spread the joy around. You are aware you have received something wonderful and, in a spontaneous upswelling of the heart want to give back a measure of the bounty. There are all kinds of ways to do that, of course, from spontaneous acts of kindness, such as letting in the car that's trying to nose in ahead of you, to planned giving such as a charitable donation.

But one of my favorite ways is something I call Dedicate This Moment: When you are enjoying something thoroughly and feeling thankful to be enjoying it, send the positive energy of that moment to someone in need. People I know have sent happy moments dancing to those who are paralyzed, moments of freedom to those suffering in prison, and moments of claiming themselves to those who have been abused. You can send energy from any positive experience for which you are grateful. I always ask my friends to send me moments when they are lying on a beach somewhere as I work, and I always send the gratitude I feel at having meaningful work to those who have thankless, boring jobs.

Dedicate This Moment operates on the principle that all of life is, in some inexplicable way, connected, and that what happens to one part—say, me—can somehow affect another part—you. It operates a lot, I think, like praying for someone; the positive energy generated can actually affect someone else's health and well-being. My favorite verification for the efficacy of prayer is studies that showed people could affect whether or not bacteria and mold grew in Petri dishes by praying for them. The bacteria and mold that were prayed for grew more rapidly and prolifically than those that were not.

The effects of positive energy sent across space and time has not yet been studied enough to be accepted fully by the scientific mind. But do we need to wait for proof before giving this a try? After all, it certainly can do no harm, and if we are able to help others feel better through our sense of gratitude, wouldn't that be absolutely wonderful?

Give Thanks for Your Body

Just to be is a blessing. Just to live is holy.

—RABBI ABRAHAM HERSCHEL

This practice is particularly difficult for women, because our relationships with our bodies is fraught with so much difficulty and dissatisfaction. The media reinforces such an impossible and singular image for young girls and women to live up to, and places so much emphasis on appearance, that virtually none of us— even if we happen to match the ideal—comes out unscathed. Eating disorders, plastic surgery, billions spent on make-up and clothes—we all know the price that is paid. And all indications are that the obsession is spreading to boys and men, with calf and biceps implants, hair replacement, face lifts, and the use of steroids to build muscle mass on the rise.

Nothing helped me get over this issue more than a book done by photographer Francis Scavullo, in which he photographed the world's most beautiful women. There they were, page after page of breathtaking women, teamed with comments from the women themselves. Not one of them was satisfied with the way she looked. Everyone complained about something: their nose was too big, hair too thin, mouth too wide.... That's when I decided once and for all to stop being dissatisfied with the way I looked. If the world's most beautiful women couldn't be satisfied, no one could, and so I might as well get over myself.

The truth is, no matter what we look like, we are all given bodies that keep us alive, and for that fact alone they are worthy of our appreciation.

My friend Andy Bryner is the best teacher I know of how to live in a body. When he does yoga, he specifically thanks each body part for how it is doing. When he stretches his leg, for example, he says something like, "Thank you, leg, for holding me up so well when I went windsurfing this morning. I appreciate your being able to stretch this much. Perhaps some day you won't be able to go this far, and so today, I really enjoy your ability to go this far." As he stretches, he goes body part by body part, noticing with exquisite particularity what his body has done for him that day and what it is able to do in this moment, without wishing or hoping it could be different.

You can try the same thing the next time you work out. Or you can do it in bed some evening. Body part by body part, inside and out, give thanks for your incarnation: kidney, liver, lung, stomach; arms, eyes, neck, toes. Think about what each does and how well it does its job.

Honor Your Teachers

*No matter what accomplishments you
achieve, somebody helped you.*

—ALTHEA GIBSON

Who have you most learned from in your life? Your fourth-grade teacher? A college professor? Your spouse? A therapist or friend? All of the above?

No matter who we are or what we have done, as tennis great Althea Gibson reminds us, there have been those who have helped us along the way, someone who said an encouraging word at exactly the right moment, offered an insight that helped us to get unstuck, or gave us the money we needed to get started. Our culture is so individualistic and competitive that it is easy to forget that we literally accomplish nothing without the help of others.

Sometimes help doesn't come in the way we would like it. Maybe your greatest teachers were those who provided a negative example or provided a mighty obstacle to rebel against. And your greatest teachers aren't necessarily people: some folks have learned most from the animals in their lives; others from great challenge such as a physical disability or illness. Author

Carol McClelland, for example, credits her breakdown after the death of her father with her development of a whole new model of change that ultimately became her life's work.

Acknowledging the help we received along the way in our lives—no matter what form it came in—will allow our hearts to soar like a well-tuned orchestra instead of a lonely violin. When we take the time to appreciate those who have been our greatest teachers, we not only express our thanks for the learnings but feel more connected to life as a whole. We see that our lives are a journey on which we become more and more fully who we are meant to be, and that we are helped on our path by a variety of people and circumstances.

You could, today, spend a few moments thinking about who or what have been your greatest teachers. But what I like to do is to ask the question of a group of people, friends or family gathered around the table for dinner, for example. It's a wonderful way to learn something new about the people in your life—something interesting or profound or moving is always revealed, I've discovered—and to feel connected to one another. And there is something about honoring your teachers out loud, to other people, that really cements the sense of gratefulness and happiness for all you have been given.

Honor Your Ancestors

There is no house like the house of belonging.
—DAVID WHYTE

When I was in college, I used to fantasize that I sprang into life fully formed as a young woman, like Aphrodite from the seafoam. It was my way of not only repudiating patterns from my parents that I didn't want to replicate, but convincing myself that, in fact, I was incapable of repeating them. It took me decades to acknowledge that while I am indeed my own unique self, I am also the child of my parents, and that indeed I am, for good and bad, more like them than I ever imagined.

It's a paradox. Here we are, a singular, irreplaceable soul here for its own purpose and, at the same time, the somewhat inevitable result of our parents and their physical and emotional legacy. We're the miraculous result of a once-in-a-lifetime meeting of a sperm and an egg, the inheritor of a particular blend of two strands of DNA and a unique personality from not only that DNA, but from all the experiences and training we had from our parents as children, as well as our particular, idiosyncratic reaction to those experiences. And our parents are in the same boat. They are the inheritors, both genetically and circumstantially, from their parents, and their parents from theirs, back throughout time. Thus, in a very real sense, we are the product of all those who came before us.

Because so many of us came from painful or difficult childhood circumstances, it is easy to either deny our connection to those who preceded us or else to blame those circumstances and our relatives for all that goes on in our lives. In either case we get stuck—first, by repeating the past because we fail to acknowledge it; second, by repeating the past because we fail to grow beyond it.

But when we take the time to really give thanks to our ancestors, we place them in their proper context, granting them neither more nor less than their due. We are able to use the lessons they have taught us (even if by negative example) and move beyond their legacy to claim our rightful place in the world. We recognize our deep connection and inhabit fully the "house of belonging."

Dawna Markova has a wonderful practice to make this real for you. "Look in the palm of your hand. Thich Nhat Hanh would say that if you look deeply enough, you'll never be lonely. Each cell of your hand is made from genetic material passed on to you from your mother and father. Whether you adored or despised them, there they are in the palm of your hand. If you look a little deeper, you'll also see your grandfathers and grandmothers. Deeper still, and there are all your ancestors resting snugly in your DNA. Can you hear them whispering in your ear, 'Maybe this is the one who will carry our dreams into the world, maybe this is the one who will move beyound the limitations that have held us back and carry our dreams into the world.'"

Honoring our connection to those who came before us gives us a sense of belonging and wholeness.

151

Send Thanksgiving Cards

*For more than thirty years, my family has sent
Thanksgiving cards rather than Christmas cards to
our friends, desiring to spread our gratitude
for the many gifts of life.*

—JOHN MARKS TEMPLETON

What a great idea! Rather than sending a Christmas card, a holiday letter listing all our accomplishments or a rote greeting, what if we took the time to catalog the things we are grateful for and tell people about those! Wouldn't it feel wonderful to open your mailbox and have a card from a friend thanking you for being in her life? Wouldn't it feel great to be the person who sends such a card?

It doesn't matter what season or event we choose—Thanksgiving, Christmas, birthdays—only that we begin to express our feelings of appreciation and gratitude. We all hunger for the connection such heartfelt appreciation creates. Richard Louv, a columnist for the *San Diego Union Tribune* and author of *The Web of Life* once wrote a column about a family that, instead of presents, gives Christmas love letters to one another each year, listing twenty-five reasons why the person receiving the letter is loved or valued. It is his most widely requested column, and the idea has been picked up by a radio station in Los Angeles. "I decided that my family had better get on board, too," he writes in *The Web of Life*.

"My list for Kathy, to whom I have been married for seventeen years, included: 'You gave birth to Matthew and Jason. You care deeply about your patients at work. You're honorable in every part of your life. I trust you. You don't pick up my socks. You took care of my mother, and me, when she was dying. You go family camping when you'd rather get room service. You introduced me to the joys of room service. You read better books that I do. The scent of your clothes. The way you look when the covers are wrapped around your face. . . .'"

"I'm looking forward to giving these lists and to receiving mine. Perhaps your family could try it too. It's just an idea; life's short."

Give Thanks at Meals

Before you taste anything, recite a blessing.
—RABBI AKIVA

As a young girl raised Catholic, I always said grace before eating. After I left the church, however, like many people who have withdrawn from organized religion, I dropped the practice of giving thanks before eating. Since I no longer believed in "God," why should I give thanks? One Thanksgiving, almost twenty-five years later, the impoverishment of this attitude struck me: Even if there was no God—and by now I was less sure—I was being given something, by farmworkers and grocery clerks and the labors of many others, and I should at least acknowledge that. The result was *A Grateful Heart: Daily Blessings for the Evening Meal from Buddha to the Beatles.* In it, I collected 365 ways to give thanks, many of them not prayers in the traditional sense.

In putting that book together I learned many things. One was how important it was, for me at least, to say something different every day (or almost every day). The problem with the grace from my childhood was that we always said the same one, and therefore, like the

Pledge of Allegiance, it lost all its meaning. Variety keeps me awake to meaning.

Mostly I discovered how crucial it is to have a daily ritual of thanksgiving to keep our eyes of appreciation open. It doesn't have to be around eating; many people report that they use *A Grateful Heart* on going to sleep or waking. But the fact that you do it every day at a set time creates a habit of the heart that makes it easier to be thankful all day long.

That being said, I do want to put in a plug for grace before meals, whether you are eating alone or with other people. One of gratitude's most important gifts is fostering a sense of connection. And eating is something that all living things do. When we eat with awareness, with thanksgiving, we strengthen our connection with the rest of life by acknowledging all the living beings that have given their lives so that we might be nourished.

We also strengthen our connection to one another. Rather than sitting in front of a TV, mindlessly shoving food into our mouths, when we sit around a table and say a prayer before eating we connect to one another in our family. We acknowledge that we are sharing this experience, and the acknowledgment itself binds us more firmly together. You can take turns reading something, or speaking spontaneously, or reciting your family's blessing. But whatever you choose to do, when you give thanks before eating, you recognize that you are together, and together, you are a part of something larger than yourselves.

157

Say "Thank You" as Often as Possible

Let's feel the magic of those two little,
big words, "thank you."

—ARDATH RODALE

This practice is very simple. Just say the words "Thank you" as often as possible. Thank you to the toll-taker for taking your money. Thank you to your coworker for bringing in the cookies. Thank you to your friend for calling on a dreary Saturday. That's all— no need to go into a big, long explanation of why you are appreciative. Just a simple, "Thank you."

In truth, this "rote" response we all learned as manners is no small thing. As Daphne Rose Kingma points out in *True Love*, saying, "[Thank you]...anchors in our minds the fact that we've been given to...creates an internal attitude of optimism...and is a character building act...[that] develops a positive view of...the world." In other words, when we say, "Thank you," we are reminded that we have been given something in this moment, which helps us remember that good things do happen to us and trust that our needs will be provided for in general.

It also has wonderful effects on the people who

receive the thank you. It makes them realize that their efforts, whatever they are, have been noticed and appreciated. And we all have a need to be appreciated. Indeed, several people who have worked for me over the years have said that they are at least as much motivated by appreciation as they are by money, and I think that's true for a lot more folks than might admit it.

Saying "Thank you" also goes a long way toward encouraging more of the same behavior in the future. We may not do something to get thanked, but being thanked makes us want to do it again. I realized that recently when I brought roses from my garden into the office and placed one in every person's office. All but one person thanked me, and I notice that my desire to do it again for her is not nearly as strong as it is to do it for everyone else. It's not that I am holding a grudge; my thinking goes more like this: "If she didn't like it, it makes no sense to do it again."

In a recent article in *Prevention*, Ardath Rodale suggests that readers count the numbers of "Thank you"s they say during one day. I think that's a great idea. So today, count your "Thank you"s. They'll probably increase by virtue of your turning your attention to them.

ℒeave a Trail of Happiness

[Appreciation] makes immortal all that is best and most beautiful. . . . It exalts the beauty of that which is beautiful. . . . It strips the veil of familiarity from the world, and lays bare and naked sleeping beauty, which is in the spirit of its forms.

—PERCY BYSSHE SHELLEY

Two of the most joy-filled people I know are Joel and Michelle Levey. They seem literally to glow from the inside with the light of vitality and love. One of the greatest things about them is how exquisitely they give thanks for whatever is done for them. I've seen the letter they sent to their publicist after a recent book tour. They thanked her so eloquently and personally that she cried. When I asked them about the letter, they said they make it a habit to thank in writing people who treat them well. "In our professional corporate work," they write, "we really value the help and support of reliable, qualified capable people." So they not only let the person know how grateful they are, but they tell the person's boss as well.

As a consequence of such a practice, wherever they

go, Joel and Michelle leave a trail of happiness, from the ticket agent at Alaska Airlines, to the waitress who served them with a smile, and the mechanic who fixed their car. Because they try not to take anything for granted, their eyes are open to the gift in the most ordinary situations, and by thanking people for those gifts, they spread the gift around.

You don't necessarily have to send letters (although a card or letter is particularly meaningful to many people, especially these days when the mailbox seems to contain only junk mail and bills). A telephone call or e-mail message will also work.

It's not just strangers and people who do work for you who would appreciate such attention. I know someone who periodically calls up friends and family out of the blue simply to tell them what she appreciates about them. She doesn't do it to get love, she does it out of an overflowing sense of gratitude that they are in her life. And, as you might expect, she is greatly loved as a consequence.

When I think of doing this, I know it's a great idea, but I'm afraid I don't have time to do it (although I feel guilty even admitting that). If you feel the same way, how about trying, after reading this, to send *one* letter or make *one* call? I plan to.

Write a "Thank You" to Yourself

It is man's foremost duty to awaken the understanding
of the inner Self and to know his own real inner
greatness. Once he knows his true worth,
he can know the worth of others.

—SWAMI MUKTANANDA

You are amazing, original, the one and only you. You think unique thoughts, express yourself in particular ways, and offer yourself to family and friends in ways that only you can. But I bet you aren't even aware of your beauty, your sensitivity, your quirky outlook on the world. In some ways, it's not possible *not* to take ourselves for granted—the way we are is just natural to us, and therefore it's hard for us to see just how marvelously wonderful we are.

That's what's so great about friends: they notice what's wonderful and point it out, and suddenly it becomes visible to us too. I'm not even aware, for example, that I have a sense of humor until my friend Rick laughs at something I've said and proclaims, "You're the funniest person I know." Other people may take their kind attentiveness to others for granted, or their creativity, or their precision. Whatever is our own gift, chances are we haven't noticed it.

When we're practicing gratitude, it's easy to notice all the things outside of ourselves we are grateful for—love and friendship and food and laughter—and forget to shine the light of appreciation on ourselves. But we all have splendid qualities, and if we learn to appreciate ourselves, our sense of gratefulness for our own beings will be magnified and our tendency to notice all our flaws and failings will diminish.

Giving thanks for all our wonderful qualities is one of the ways we learn truly to love ourselves. From that self-love, we can then feel worthy of love from others and have strong, healthy relationships. Because we feel worthy, we can love without being overly demanding, clinging, or rejecting.

Today, try writing a note of thanks to yourself. It can be for anything that you feel grateful to yourself for—being a good friend, for example, or working hard, or dressing with flair. Take the time to think of as many things you are grateful to yourself for as possible. Doesn't it bring a warm smile to your face to think of how marvelous you are?

Fall in Love Again and Again

Choose thy love. Love thy choice.

—GERMAN PROVERB

Why is it that we can be so kind, tolerant, and loving to people we barely know and so demanding, cold, and downright mean to those who are the closest to us? Somehow, by virtue of daily exposure, all the wonderful traits in your beloved that attracted you in the first place become invisible, and every flaw and imperfection looms large. We get so focused on all that we want from our partner but don't have that we can't see the beautiful person who is available to us in this present moment.

I once knew a therapist who claimed that she had discovered a whole new way to improve relationships. Rather than having couples or parents and kids talk out their problems, she claimed that she had better results from having people send a loving, grateful thought to the other person every time they felt themselves getting annoyed or angry. I tried it at home. When I found myself about to say to my husband, "Why can't you say something interesting?" I would instead focus on something I was grateful for: "I love the way he treats people so

THE PRACTICES
OF GRATITUDE

gently." What was amazing, was how everything changed. He got more interesting and more loving. Now, whether it was because I changed my attitude and we were not fighting or being caught in hurt feelings, or that my blessing him actually enhanced those qualities in him, I can't say. Nor, frankly, does it matter. The point is that appreciating the good made the good blossom.

Noticing what you love is a mental habit that anyone can learn. Hypnotherapist Milton Erickson used to teach this practice. He said he could get anyone to fall in and out of love with anyone else. All you do is this. Look at a person and find five things you can't stand, for example, their laugh, the way they smell, the way they put down someone, the fact they make a mess when eating, the scum on their teeth. Then find five things you love: the shape of their hands, their big blue eyes, their generosity with material objects, their sense of humor, the way they speak to their kids. For one week, every time you meet someone, do this practice. Soon you'll discover that you *can* affect the way you feel toward someone by choosing to focus on what you like.

Then bring this ability home. Become an expert at switching from negative to positive when you find yourself on a mental rant about your mate, and see what happens in your life.

Appreciate Your Kids Just as They Are

Thank you for being.

—Traditional greeting of the Seneca

As parents, we can get so focused on everything our kids need to learn, to change, to become, that we forget to appreciate them right now for who they are. This is especially true these days, when life is more competitive than ever. We want the best for our children— we want them to have a good education, excel in sports, have friends. We want them to get into a good college, make a good marriage, be wonderful parents of their own. Focused on all we want for them, we can become preoccupied by their faults, their shortcomings, their lacks. If only Johnny could read better, if only Claudia would sit still, if only Yolanda wasn't so shy. . . .

For the most part, schools help reinforce our fixation on what's wrong, for they have become specialists in diagnosing problems and affixing labels: hyperactive, attention deficit, oppositional, unmotivated. Everyone tells us so much about what's wrong with our kids that it's easy to lose track of our love and appreciation.

My friend Molly has six kids, ranging from twenty-five to eight, all of whom, while very different, have for the most part a healthy sense of self-esteem. Each in his or her own way is blossoming. They do well in school, some better than others. They play sports, some better than others. They have friends, some more than others. They all love one another and their parents a tremendous amount. When I see Molly interact with them, I think I know part of the reason why. She tells them often that they are wonderful just the way they are, that they are loved right now in this moment without changing or improving. No comparing with siblings, no pushing to be better.

What if we greeted our children like the Seneca, saying "Thank you for being" when they woke in the morning or went to sleep at night? What would change for them to feel our gratitude for their being without having to do anything? What would change for us?

ℒive as if Every Day Is Your Last

Buddha said that fortune changes like the swish of
a horse's tail. Tomorrow could be the first day of thirty
years of quadriplegia. . . . The more you open to life the less
death becomes the enemy. When you start using death as a
means of focusing on life, then everything becomes
just as it is, just this moment, an extraordinary
opportunity to be really alive.

—STEPHEN LEVINE

Whether it is right or not, sometimes it is only the possibility of our not being here on Earth anymore that wakes us up to the beauty of our lives. That's one of the reasons Buddhists contemplate their own death—to awaken to the joy that is available in the present moment.

If this *were* your last day on Earth, would you worry about the clutter in your house or the state of your thighs? I'll bet not. Chances are you'd use the time to memorize your baby's smile, the smell of your Sterling Silver roses, the feeling of the rain as it pelts the top of your head. If this were the last day on Earth of someone you loved, would you spend the time arguing about whose turn it is to take out the garbage or who's right about where to send your child to school? More likely you'd spend the time telling him or her how much you love them and how grateful you are for all they have done for you.

The truth is, of course, that today might be our last day on Earth, because the future is never guaranteed. Too many people go out of the house blithely one day and never return—victims of car accidents, heart attacks, drive-by shootings, plane crashes, and other catastrophes of living—for any of us to take our continued existence for granted.

The purpose of living as if each day were our last is not to create an overwrought sense of having to grab every experience right now. Nor is it an excuse to ignore the garbage that needs to go out, the bills that need to be paid, the clutter that needs to be picked up. Rather it is merely a reminder to be present to our lives as they unfold, to take in, as much as we can, our daily existence.

Thich Nhat Hanh has a wonderful meditation for this, called The Hugging Meditation. It's very simple— all you do is hug someone three times, breathing in and out with awareness. The first time, you both think about how at some time, you don't know when, you will no longer be here. The second time, you focus on how, at some time, you don't know when, the other person will no longer be here. The third time, you truly take in that you are both here now, together in this precious moment.

I try to do it with my husband and daughter whenever I am to be away for any significant length of time, but my new goal is to do it every morning before I walk out the door.

171

THE PRACTICES
OF GRATITUDE

THE DEEPENING JOURNEY

What amazes me is that before we can count we are taught to be grateful for what others do. As we are broken open by our experience, we begin to be grateful for what is, and if we live long enough and deep enough and authentically enough, gratitude becomes a way of life.

—MARK NEPO

Y NOW I HOPE YOU'VE COME TO EXPERIENCE some of the great joy gratitude can bring, and have begun to see that the attitudes and practices of gratitude lead us on a soul-journey, one that the preceding quote by poet and cancer survivor Mark Nepo so perfectly describes. Gratitude begins with training in what we call manners, a learned response to being on the receiving end of a human transaction: "Mrs. Smith just gave you a cookie, Janey. Now what do you say?" Despite the benefits of such thanks, they are contingent on someone doing something specific for us, and while many of us remain at this level of gratitude, our souls call out for us to move to a deeper level.

Here we begin to discover gratitude apart from a specific human giver, apart from roses on Valentine's Day and the CD player on Christmas, and acknowledge the gift of life itself. Here we begin to be appreciative of everything, as teachers along our soul's path. This second level of gratitude is most often found through suffering, by choosing to get soft and wide, rather than rigid and pointy, under the yoke of life's difficulties.

When we allow ourselves to be broken open by life rather than broken down by it, we begin to be grateful for the difficulties themselves—to cancer for bringing us to our feelings; to bankruptcy for saving us from the rat race; to a demanding person for teaching us how to stand up for ourselves.

When we live from this place long enough, we begin actually to inhabit gratitude, our every inhalation and exhalation a breath of thanksgiving no matter what is going on in the external world. Not many travelers make it all the way here permanently; this is the territory of saints. But all of us experience this spot in glimpses, moments in which we look up at the sky and see it for the work of art that it is; hear Beethoven's *Ninth* and feel the majestic surprise of such music in our lives; feel our baby's pudgy fingers on our face and cry tears of thanks for her being.

At each level of gratitude, our soul's capacity deepens. At the first level, we experience contentment—we wanted a cookie and we got it. At the second, we experience meaning—we're here for a purpose and are therefore grateful for all of life's lessons. At the third, we dwell in pure joy, "the simple response of our heart to this given life in all its fullness," as Brother David Steindl-Rast puts it.

May you experience all the levels of thankfulness and the soul-gifts that each offers. For then it will be truly possible to give and receive joy every day of your life.

THE
DEEPENING
JOURNEY

The Unleashed Power of God's Word

As Paul discoursed on righteousness, self-control and the judgment to come, Felix was afraid (Acts 24:25).

The prisoner: Paul. The judge: Felix.
Yet Paul had Felix right where he wanted him!
Sitting in judgment on Paul's case, Felix became the unsuspecting target of Paul's gospel.
The accused stands before the judge . . . but it is the judge who is convicted! It's a remarkable turn of events that John Calvin explores.

Walk With John Calvin

"Now Felix is forced to realize the effectiveness of the Word of God, a power of which he had no concept. This man, who held the power of life and death over Paul, is trembling all over, as if he were standing before his own judge.

"Forgetting that he is a prisoner bound in chains, Paul exercises the judgment of heaven in the name of Christ. Because he is aware that he must speak in the name of Christ, Paul does not submit to human authority; but, as if from a higher level, he carries out the mission entrusted him by God.

"Let us learn from this what a great influence the Spirit of God exercised not only in Paul's heart but also in his tongue.

"The Word of God has not been bound along with Paul, for not only did he declare it freely and boldly, but it penetrated the hearts of men—proud in their greatness—as if lightning flashed out of heaven."

Walk Closer to God

The same Word of God that fortified Paul terrified Felix. Why?
Because "the Word of God is living and active. Sharper than any double-edged sword, it penetrates even to dividing soul and spirit, joints and marrow; it judges the thoughts and attitudes of the heart" (Hebrews 4:12).

Circumstances cannot shackle the power of the Word—a power demonstrated every time a human voice declares it. A voice like yours—telling what you know is true with boldness only the Spirit can give.

MAY 28

 Walk in the Word
Acts 25

Two years elapse, a new governor sits in Caesarea, and a new trial begins; an indecisive Festus suggests a Jerusalem trial, to which Paul responds with an appeal to Caesar.

The Trial Before Festus

25 Three days after arriving in the province, Festus went up from Caesarea to Jerusalem, ²where the chief priests and Jewish leaders appeared before him and presented the charges against Paul. ³They urgently requested Festus, as a favor to them, to have Paul transferred to Jerusalem, for they were preparing an ambush to kill him along the way. ⁴Festus answered, "Paul is being held at Caesarea, and I myself am going there soon. ⁵Let some of your leaders come with me and press charges against the man there, if he has done anything wrong."

⁶After spending eight or ten days with them, he went down to Caesarea, and the next day he convened the court and ordered that Paul be brought before him. ⁷When Paul appeared, the Jews who had come down from Jerusalem stood around him, bringing many serious charges against him, which they could not prove.

⁸Then Paul made his defense: "I have done nothing wrong against the law of the Jews or against the temple or against Caesar."

⁹Festus, wishing to do the Jews a favor, said to Paul, "Are you willing to go up to Jerusalem and stand trial before me there on these charges?"

¹⁰Paul answered: "I am now standing before Caesar's court, where I ought to be tried. I have not done any wrong to the Jews, as you yourself know very well. ¹¹If, however, I am guilty of doing anything deserving death, I do not refuse to die. But if the charges brought against me by these Jews are not true, no one has the right to hand me over to them. I appeal to Caesar!"

¹²After Festus had conferred with his council, he declared: "You have appealed to Caesar. To Caesar you will go!"

Festus Consults King Agrippa

¹³A few days later King Agrippa and Bernice arrived at Caesarea to pay their respects to Festus. ¹⁴Since they were spending many days there, Festus discussed Paul's case with the king. He said: "There is a man here whom Felix left as a prisoner. ¹⁵When I went to Jerusalem, the chief priests and elders of the Jews brought charges against him and asked that he be condemned.

¹⁶"I told them that it is not the Roman custom to hand over any man before he has faced his accusers and has had an opportunity to defend himself against their charges. ¹⁷When they came here with me, I did not delay the case, but convened the court the next day and ordered the man to be brought in. ¹⁸When his accusers got up to speak, they did not charge him with any of the crimes I had expected. ¹⁹Instead, they had some points

MAY 28

of dispute with him about their own religion and about a dead man named Jesus who Paul claimed was alive. ²⁰I was at a loss how to investigate such matters; so I asked if he would be willing to go to Jerusalem and stand trial there on these charges. ²¹When Paul made his appeal to be held over for the Emperor's decision, I ordered him held until I could send him to Caesar."

²²Then Agrippa said to Festus, "I would like to hear this man myself." He replied, "Tomorrow you will hear him."

Paul Before Agrippa

²³The next day Agrippa and Bernice came with great pomp and entered the audience room with the high ranking officers and the leading men of the city. At the command of Festus, Paul was brought in. ²⁴Festus said: "King Agrippa, and all who are present with us, you see this man! The whole Jewish community has petitioned me about him in Jerusalem and here in Caesarea, shouting that he ought not to live any longer. ²⁵I found he had done nothing deserving of death, but because he made his appeal to the Emperor I decided to send him to Rome. ²⁶But I have nothing definite to write to His Majesty about him. Therefore I have brought him before all of you, and especially before you, King Agrippa, so that as a result of this investigation I may have something to write. ²⁷For I think it is unreasonable to send on a prisoner without specifying the charges against him."

PSALM 86

A prayer of David.

Hear, O LORD, and answer me,
for I am poor and needy.
²Guard my life, for I am devoted to you.
You are my God; save your servant
who trusts in you.
³Have mercy on me, O Lord,
for I call to you all day long.
⁴Bring joy to your servant,
for to you, O Lord,
I lift up my soul.

⁵You are forgiving and good, O Lord,
abounding in love to all who call to you.
⁶Hear my prayer, O LORD;
listen to my cry for mercy.
⁷In the day of my trouble I will call to you,
for you will answer me.

MAY 28

The Guarantee of the Believer's Resurrection

Instead, they had some points of dispute with him about their own religion and about a dead man named Jesus who Paul claimed was alive (Acts 25:19).

Believing in Christ's resurrection cost Paul a lot. He was imprisoned, flogged, exposed to death, stoned and shipwrecked. He was in danger from rivers, bandits, Jews, Gentiles and false Christians. He went without sleep, food, drink, warmth and clothing. Besides all that, he was "stressed-out" with concern for his flock like any good pastor. Now he was in chains, defending himself before King Agrippa.

R.L. Dabney explains the importance of and evidence for this cardinal doctrine of Christianity.

Walk With R.L. Dabney

"Christ's resurrection is everywhere spoken of in Scripture as a hinge point of the believer's salvation and hope. The apostles everywhere put it forth as the main point of their testimony. It may be proved by the following:

"First, from Old Testament predictions such as Psalm 16:10. This event is one of the criteria predicted for the Messiah. Once you have proved that Jesus is the expected Messiah, you may claim that a resurrection is to be expected for him.

"Second, Christ expressly predicted his own resurrection (Matthew 20:19; 27:63; and John 10:18). If he is not a monstrous imposter, which his lovely character disproves, we must expect to find it true.

"Third, we have the testimony of many witnesses who saw him after his rising—the eleven, the five-hundred, and last of all Paul. These were competent, honest and credible witnesses. They had everything to lose, and nothing to gain by bearing false testimony on this.

"Fourth, miracles were wrought in its confirmation. The outpouring of the Spirit at Pentecost and all the following outpourings are proofs of it, for they are fruits of his ascension.

"The resurrection of Christ is the guarantee and proof of ours."

Walk Closer to God

Yes, believing in Christ's resurrection cost Paul a lot. But not believing in Christ's resurrection will cost so many so much more.

Be like Paul today—talk to someone about that momentous event. ◖

MAY 29

Walk in the Word
Acts 26

Before sending Paul to Caesar, Festus takes advantage of King Agrippa's presence in Caesarea to ask his advice and have him listen to Paul, who once again tells his life story and testimony; Luke reports Agrippa's conclusion that Paul is innocent.

26 Then Agrippa said to Paul, "You have permission to speak for yourself."

So Paul motioned with his hand and began his defense: ²"King Agrippa, I consider myself fortunate to stand before you today as I make my defense against all the accusations of the Jews, ³and especially so because you are well acquainted with all the Jewish customs and controversies. Therefore, I beg you to listen to me patiently.

⁴"The Jews all know the way I have lived ever since I was a child, from the beginning of my life in my own country, and also in Jerusalem. ⁵They have known me for a long time and can testify, if they are willing, that according to the strictest sect of our religion, I lived as a Pharisee. ⁶And now it is because of my hope in what God has promised our fathers that I am on trial today. ⁷This is the promise our twelve tribes are hoping to see fulfilled as they earnestly serve God day and night. O king, it is because of this hope that the Jews are accusing me. ⁸Why should any of you consider it incredible that God raises the dead?

⁹"I too was convinced that I ought to do all that was possible to oppose the name of Jesus of Nazareth. ¹⁰And that is just what I did in Jerusalem. On the authority of the chief priests I put many of the saints in prison, and when they were put to death, I cast my vote against them. ¹¹Many a time I went from one synagogue to another to have them punished, and I tried to force them to blaspheme. In my obsession against them, I even went to foreign cities to persecute them.

¹²"On one of these journeys I was going to Damascus with the authority and commission of the chief priests. ¹³About noon, O king, as I was on the road, I saw a light from heaven, brighter than the sun, blazing around me and my companions. ¹⁴We all fell to the ground, and I heard a voice saying to me in Aramaic,ᵃ 'Saul, Saul, why do you persecute me? It is hard for you to kick against the goads.'

¹⁵"Then I asked, 'Who are you, Lord?'

" 'I am Jesus, whom you are persecuting,' the Lord replied. ¹⁶'Now get up and stand on your feet. I have appeared to you to appoint you as a servant and as a witness of what you have seen of me and what I will show you. ¹⁷I will rescue you from your own people and from the Gentiles. I am sending you to them ¹⁸to open their eyes and turn them from darkness to light, and from the power of Satan to God, so that they may receive forgiveness of sins and a place among those who are sanctified by faith in me.'

¹⁹"So then, King Agrippa, I was not disobedient to the vision from heaven. ²⁰First to those in Damascus, then to those in Jerusalem and in all

MAY 29

Judea, and to the Gentiles also, I preached that they should repent and turn to God and prove their repentance by their deeds. [21]That is why the Jews seized me in the temple courts and tried to kill me. [22]But I have had God's help to this very day, and so I stand here and testify to small and great alike. I am saying nothing beyond what the prophets and Moses said would happen— [23]that the Christ[b] would suffer and, as the first to rise from the dead, would proclaim light to his own people and to the Gentiles."

[24]At this point Festus interrupted Paul's defense. "You are out of your mind, Paul!" he shouted. "Your great learning is driving you insane."

[25]"I am not insane, most excellent Festus," Paul replied. "What I am saying is true and reasonable. [26]The king is familiar with these things, and I can speak freely to him. I am convinced that none of this has escaped his notice, because it was not done in a corner. [27]King Agrippa, do you believe the prophets? I know you do."

[28]Then Agrippa said to Paul, "Do you think that in such a short time you can persuade me to be a Christian?"

[29]Paul replied, "Short time or long—I pray God that not only you but all who are listening to me today may become what I am, except for these chains."

[30]The king rose, and with him the governor and Bernice and those sitting with them. [31]They left the room, and while talking with one another, they said, "This man is not doing anything that deserves death or imprisonment."

[32]Agrippa said to Festus, "This man could have been set free if he had not appealed to Caesar."

[a]14 Or *Hebrew*   [b]23 Or *Messiah*

Worship From The HEART

Paul didn't mince words before King Agrippa as he told the exciting story of his conversion and the dramatic change in his life. Take time to remember the occasion when you met Jesus and accepted him as Savior. Tell God how exciting that event was, and in your own words tell him how and why your love for him has deepened since then.

The Only Life-and-Death Decision

 Then Agrippa said to Paul, "Do you think that in such a short time you can persuade me to be a Christian?" (Acts 26:28).

People feel intense pressure when they are discussing issues that are life and death—especially if their own lifestyles are at stake. This is why discussions about Christ can be so intense. Christ's message to the unbeliever is, "Your way of life is hellish. I am your only hope." People are intensely uncomfortable with that.

When Paul preached to Agrippa, he turned the pressure to full steam. Agrippa reacted like so many do under the pressure of the truth: He squirmed. He protested. He procrastinated. He escaped.

Matthew Henry explains why.

Walk With Matthew Henry

"Agrippa could not but agree that the Old Testament prophecies found their fulfillment in Christ.

"And now that Paul urges him solemnly, he is nearly ready to yield to the conviction of the Spirit.

"He sees a great deal of reason for Christianity. The proofs of it, he admits, are strong; the objections against it, trifling.

"If it were not for his obligations to tradition, his respect for the religion of his fathers and of his country, his regard to his dignity as a king, and his secular interests, he would turn to Christianity immediately. Many are almost persuaded to be saved, who are not quite persuaded.

"They are under strong convictions of their duty, and of the excellency of the ways of God, yet are overruled by some outward circumstances, and do not pursue their convictions."

Walk Closer to God

King Agrippa's symptoms: shortsighted vision, a tendency to sacrifice conviction for convenience, and a preoccupation with worldly affairs and popular approval.

The only known cure for such a condition? Taking Jesus Christ at his Word—the same Christ whom the apostle Paul proclaimed.

It was a life-and-death decision—perhaps the very one you are wrestling with today. Agrippa knew the cure, but wasn't willing to take it. Are you? ◖▯

MAY 30

Walk in the Word
Acts 27

From the vantage point of an eyewitness, Luke tells the story of the trip to Rome, which was disrupted by a raging storm that ruined the ship.

Paul Sails for Rome

27 When it was decided that we would sail for Italy, Paul and some other prisoners were handed over to a centurion named Julius, who belonged to the Imperial Regiment. ²We boarded a ship from Adramyttium about to sail for ports along the coast of the province of Asia, and we put out to sea. Aristarchus, a Macedonian from Thessalonica, was with us.

³The next day we landed at Sidon; and Julius, in kindness to Paul, allowed him to go to his friends so they might provide for his needs. ⁴From there we put out to sea again and passed to the lee of Cyprus because the winds were against us. ⁵When we had sailed across the open sea off the coast of Cilicia and Pamphylia, we landed at Myra in Lycia. ⁶There the centurion found an Alexandrian ship sailing for Italy and put us on board. ⁷We made slow headway for many days and had difficulty arriving off Cnidus. When the wind did not allow us to hold our course, we sailed to the lee of Crete, opposite Salmone. ⁸We moved along the coast with difficulty and came to a place called Fair Havens, near the town of Lasea.

⁹Much time had been lost, and sailing had already become dangerous because by now it was after the Fast.ᵃ So Paul warned them, ¹⁰"Men, I can see that our voyage is going to be disastrous and bring great loss to ship and cargo, and to our own lives also." ¹¹But the centurion, instead of listening to what Paul said, followed the advice of the pilot and of the owner of the ship. ¹²Since the harbor was unsuitable to winter in, the majority decided that we should sail on, hoping to reach Phoenix and winter there. This was a harbor in Crete, facing both southwest and northwest.

The Storm

¹³When a gentle south wind began to blow, they thought they had obtained what they wanted; so they weighed anchor and sailed along the shore of Crete. ¹⁴Before very long, a wind of hurricane force, called the "northeaster," swept down from the island. ¹⁵The ship was caught by the storm and could not head into the wind; so we gave way to it and were driven along. ¹⁶As we passed to the lee of a small island called Cauda, we were hardly able to make the lifeboat secure. ¹⁷When the men had hoisted it aboard, they passed ropes under the ship itself to hold it together. Fearing that they would run aground on the sandbars of Syrtis, they lowered the sea anchor and let the ship be driven along. ¹⁸We took such a violent battering from the storm that the next day they began to throw the cargo overboard. ¹⁹On the third day, they threw the ship's tackle overboard with

their own hands. 20When neither sun nor stars appeared for many days and the storm continued raging, we finally gave up all hope of being saved.

21After the men had gone a long time without food, Paul stood up before them and said: "Men, you should have taken my advice not to sail from Crete; then you would have spared yourselves this damage and loss. 22But now I urge you to keep up your courage, because not one of you will be lost; only the ship will be destroyed. 23Last night an angel of the God whose I am and whom I serve stood beside me 24and said, 'Do not be afraid, Paul. You must stand trial before Caesar; and God has graciously given you the lives of all who sail with you.' 25So keep up your courage, men, for I have faith in God that it will happen just as he told me. 26Nevertheless, we must run aground on some island."

The Shipwreck

27On the fourteenth night we were still being driven across the Adriatic*b* Sea, when about midnight the sailors sensed they were approaching land. 28They took soundings and found that the water was a hundred and twenty feet*c* deep. A short time later they took soundings again and found it was ninety feet*d* deep. 29Fearing that we would be dashed against the rocks, they dropped four anchors from the stern and prayed for daylight. 30In an attempt to escape from the ship, the sailors let the lifeboat down into the sea, pretending they were going to lower some anchors from the bow. 31Then Paul said to the centurion and the soldiers, "Unless these men stay with the ship, you cannot be saved." 32So the soldiers cut the ropes that held the lifeboat and let it fall away.

33Just before dawn Paul urged them all to eat. "For the last fourteen days," he said, "you have been in constant suspense and have gone without food—you haven't eaten anything. 34Now I urge you to take some food. You need it to survive. Not one of you will lose a single hair from his head." 35After he said this, he took some bread and gave thanks to God in front of them all. Then he broke it and began to eat. 36They were all encouraged and ate some food themselves. 37Altogether there were 276 of us on board. 38When they had eaten as much as they wanted, they lightened the ship by throwing the grain into the sea.

39When daylight came, they did not recognize the land, but they saw a bay with a sandy beach, where they decided to run the ship aground if they could. 40Cutting loose the anchors, they left them in the sea and at the same time untied the ropes that held the rudders. Then they hoisted the foresail to the wind and made for the beach. 41But the ship struck a sandbar and ran aground. The bow stuck fast and would not move, and the stern was broken to pieces by the pounding of the surf.

42The soldiers planned to kill the prisoners to prevent any of them from swimming away and escaping. 43But the centurion wanted to spare Paul's

MAY 30

life and kept them from carrying out their plan. He ordered those who could swim to jump overboard first and get to land. [44]The rest were to get there on planks or on pieces of the ship. In this way everyone reached land in safety.

[a]9 That is, the Day of Atonement (Yom Kippur)   [b]27 In ancient times the name referred to an area extending well south of Italy.   [c]28 Greek *twenty orguias* (about 37 meters)   [d]28 Greek *fifteen orguias* (about 27 meters)

PSALM 121

A song of ascents.

I lift up my eyes to the hills—
    where does my help come from?
[2]My help comes from the LORD,
    the Maker of heaven and earth.

[3]He will not let your foot slip—
    he who watches over you will not slumber;
[4]indeed, he who watches over Israel
    will neither slumber nor sleep.

[5]The LORD watches over you—
    the LORD is your shade at your right hand;
[6]the sun will not harm you by day,
    nor the moon by night.

[7]The LORD will keep you from all harm—
    he will watch over your life;
[8]the LORD will watch over your coming and going
    both now and forevermore.

MAY 30

Ready for Teachable Moments

Much time had been lost, and sailing had already become dangerous. . . . So Paul warned them (Acts 27:9).

Who needs a Savior when the sun is shining brightly, the sea is calm and the sails are moved by a serene and gentle breeze?

But let the storms of life break loose and trials wash around like high waves, and suddenly the self-sufficient are looking for answers—fast! Answers that the Christian is uniquely prepared to supply, as Joseph Parker explains.

Walk With Joseph Parker

"For the Christian to speak when the ship is going merrily over the blue waves is not wrong, but perhaps not best; so the Christian waits.

"The ship comes into difficulty; the sailors begin to look despairingly at the whole situation; illness is about; the air is troubled. Now, if any of you can say a word of comfort, do say it. The Christian is waiting for these times.

"The moment the door stands ajar, he is in; the moment the opportunity shows itself, he seizes it.

"Be wise and do not speak before the time, or your words will be like good seed sown upon the fickle and noisy wind.

"The clock will strike for you—be ready when the hour comes.

"The word will keep; and when it is spoken after long delay, it will come with more thundering resonance, with more penetrating emphasis.

"For that time the Christian witness waits."

Walk Closer to God

Death. Lingering illness. Financial reversal. Broken marriage. Runaway child. Loneliness. Loss of job.

The storms of life come with sudden fury. And with them, the realization that someone bigger is needed to cope with life . . . and death.

People will reach for a Savior when they know they need to be saved. The wise witness is faithful at all times, but watchful for the teachable moments of life.

Will you be ready to speak when they are ready to listen? ()

MAY 31

 Walk in the Word
Acts 28

Luke writes of the survival of the passengers, who spent several months on Malta before sailing on to Rome, where Paul preached the gospel.

Ashore on Malta

28 Once safely on shore, we found out that the island was called Malta. ²The islanders showed us unusual kindness. They built a fire and welcomed us all because it was raining and cold. ³Paul gathered a pile of brushwood and, as he put it on the fire, a viper, driven out by the heat, fastened itself on his hand. ⁴When the islanders saw the snake hanging from his hand, they said to each other, "This man must be a murderer; for though he escaped from the sea, Justice has not allowed him to live." ⁵But Paul shook the snake off into the fire and suffered no ill effects. ⁶The people expected him to swell up or suddenly fall dead, but after waiting a long time and seeing nothing unusual happen to him, they changed their minds and said he was a god.

⁷There was an estate nearby that belonged to Publius, the chief official of the island. He welcomed us to his home and for three days entertained us hospitably. ⁸His father was sick in bed, suffering from fever and dysentery. Paul went in to see him and, after prayer, placed his hands on him and healed him. ⁹When this had happened, the rest of the sick on the island came and were cured. ¹⁰They honored us in many ways and when we were ready to sail, they furnished us with the supplies we needed.

Arrival at Rome

¹¹After three months we put out to sea in a ship that had wintered in the island. It was an Alexandrian ship with the figurehead of the twin gods Castor and Pollux. ¹²We put in at Syracuse and stayed there three days. ¹³From there we set sail and arrived at Rhegium. The next day the south wind came up, and on the following day we reached Puteoli. ¹⁴There we found some brothers who invited us to spend a week with them. And so we came to Rome. ¹⁵The brothers there had heard that we were coming, and they traveled as far as the Forum of Appius and the Three Taverns to meet us. At the sight of these men Paul thanked God and was encouraged. ¹⁶When we got to Rome, Paul was allowed to live by himself, with a soldier to guard him.

Paul Preaches at Rome Under Guard

¹⁷Three days later he called together the leaders of the Jews. When they had assembled, Paul said to them: "My brothers, although I have done nothing against our people or against the customs of our ancestors, I was arrested in Jerusalem and handed over to the Romans. ¹⁸They examined me and wanted to release me, because I was not guilty of any crime deserving death. ¹⁹But when the Jews objected, I was compelled to appeal to Caesar—not that I had any charge to bring against my own people. ²⁰For

MAY 31

this reason I have asked to see you and talk with you. It is because of the hope of Israel that I am bound with this chain."

²¹They replied, "We have not received any letters from Judea concerning you, and none of the brothers who have come from there has reported or said anything bad about you. ²²But we want to hear what your views are, for we know that people everywhere are talking against this sect."

²³They arranged to meet Paul on a certain day, and came in even larger numbers to the place where he was staying. From morning till evening he explained and declared to them the kingdom of God and tried to convince them about Jesus from the Law of Moses and from the Prophets. ²⁴Some were convinced by what he said, but others would not believe. ²⁵They disagreed among themselves and began to leave after Paul had made this final statement: "The Holy Spirit spoke the truth to your forefathers when he said through Isaiah the prophet:

²⁶" 'Go to this people and say,
"You will be ever hearing but never understanding;
    you will be ever seeing but never perceiving."
²⁷For this people's heart has become calloused;
    they hardly hear with their ears,
    and they have closed their eyes.
Otherwise they might see with their eyes,
    hear with their ears,
    understand with their hearts
and turn, and I would heal them.'ᵃ

²⁸"Therefore I want you to know that God's salvation has been sent to the Gentiles, and they will listen!"ᵇ

³⁰For two whole years Paul stayed there in his own rented house and welcomed all who came to see him. ³¹Boldly and without hindrance he preached the kingdom of God and taught about the Lord Jesus Christ.

ᵃ27 Isaiah 6:9,10   ᵇ28 Some manuscripts listen!" ²⁹After he said this, the Jews left, arguing vigorously among themselves.

May 31

God's Servants, God's Possessions

Once safely on shore . . . The islanders showed us unusual
kindness. . . . They honored us in many ways (Acts 28:1–2,10).

Persecution, danger, shipwreck, snakebite, imprisonment. Where
did Paul find the strength to face each new challenge?

Romans 8:37 will tell you in his own words.

God specializes in caring for his own as they go about the business
of heaven—a truth that J. Hudson Taylor underscores from firsthand
experience.

Walk With J. Hudson Taylor

"Even in shipwreck and uncertainty, the apostle's heart relied on the
truth that he was God's possession, as well as God's servant.

"Long before Paul's day, the assurance given in Deuteronomy 33:12
that 'the beloved of the Lord [will] rest secure in him' had conveyed rest
and confidence to many an Israelite.

"Shall we not all rest in the same blessed fact? We are his by creation,
his by redemption.

"We value and take care of our own possessions; we cherish and
protect our loved ones; how much more does he, whose love and
resources so infinitely exceed ours?

"God's love has sustained us. It is unchanging because he is
unchanging. He is the great Rock-foundation which alone cannot be
shaken.

"We know not what the future may bring with it, but we know him
who is the same yesterday, today, and forever. We put our hand afresh
in his, and say, 'Lord, lead me on.' "

Walk Closer to God

For all the hardships and uncertainties Paul faced, you can certainly
say one thing about his life.

It wasn't dull!

Yet Paul undoubtedly greeted each new day with the words, "Lord,
lead me on."

He trusted God with his future, knowing that he was already there.
But above all, Paul felt, acted, and actually was more than a conqueror
in the strength that God supplied.

That same strength is neither diluted nor diminished. And it is yours
to draw upon today. ◖

JUNE

Mining the Treasures of the Gospel

ROMANS

For generations Christians have regarded the book of Romans as one of the meatiest books of the Bible, brimming with rich theological truths. Augustine, Luther, Wesley and many other "movers and shakers" of the church trace their conversions back to a personal encounter with this "manifesto of the Christian faith." Luther went so far as to claim that Romans should become the subject of the believer's daily meditation, while Calvin maintained that someone who understood this letter would be able to understand the entire Scriptures.

But don't assume that because Romans is significant, reading it will be a simple task. Perhaps Peter was thinking of Romans when he said that some of Paul's writings were hard to understand (2 Peter 3:15–16). Think of your task in reading the book of Romans as that of a prospector mining the pages of God's Word. There is gold for you to discover each day this month.

But be sure never to forget this: Romans was not too difficult or too theological for the Holy Spirit to instruct Paul to send to Christians in Rome, many of whom were from the lower classes of Roman society and could neither read nor write. But they could, and did, study this letter sent to them by Paul. With God's help, therefore, you can understand Paul's message in Romans. It overflows with good news for Paul's day and for ours, describing "the gospel . . . the power of God for the salvation of everyone who believes" (Romans 1:16). You will be reminded of our human predicament (Romans 1–2), God's provision (Romans 3–5), God's power (Romans 6–8), God's plan (Romans 9–11) and the practical applications of your faith in Christ (Romans 12–16). Couple that with the seasoned insights of godly men and women from the past, and you are in for an inspirational month indeed! Begin mining those golden truths of Romans, guaranteed to enrich and transform your life.

JUNE 1

Walk in the Word
Romans 1:1–17

After an opening greeting, Paul expresses gratitude for the Roman Christians and a longing to visit them; he then summarizes the theme of the letter.

1 Paul, a servant of Christ Jesus, called to be an apostle and set apart for the gospel of God— ²the gospel he promised beforehand through his prophets in the Holy Scriptures ³regarding his Son, who as to his human nature was a descendant of David, ⁴and who through the Spirit*a* of holiness was declared with power to be the Son of God*b* by his resurrection from the dead: Jesus Christ our Lord. ⁵Through him and for his name's sake, we received grace and apostleship to call people from among all the Gentiles to the obedience that comes from faith. ⁶And you also are among those who are called to belong to Jesus Christ.

⁷To all in Rome who are loved by God and called to be saints:

Grace and peace to you from God our Father and from the Lord Jesus Christ.

Paul's Longing to Visit Rome

⁸First, I thank my God through Jesus Christ for all of you, because your faith is being reported all over the world. ⁹God, whom I serve with my whole heart in preaching the gospel of his Son, is my witness how constantly I remember you ¹⁰in my prayers at all times; and I pray that now at last by God's will the way may be opened for me to come to you.

¹¹I long to see you so that I may impart to you some spiritual gift to make you strong— ¹²that is, that you and I may be mutually encouraged by each other's faith. ¹³I do not want you to be unaware, brothers, that I planned many times to come to you (but have been prevented from doing so until now) in order that I might have a harvest among you, just as I have had among the other Gentiles.

¹⁴I am obligated both to Greeks and non-Greeks, both to the wise and the foolish. ¹⁵That is why I am so eager to preach the gospel also to you who are at Rome.

¹⁶I am not ashamed of the gospel, because it is the power of God for the salvation of everyone who believes: first for the Jew, then for the Gentile. ¹⁷For in the gospel a righteousness from God is revealed, a righteousness that is by faith from first to last,*c* just as it is written: "The righteous will live by faith."*d*

a4 Or *who as to his spirit*   *b4* Or *was appointed to be the Son of God with power*
c17 Or *is from faith to faith*   *d17* Hab. 2:4

The Greatest Power in the Universe

 I am not ashamed of the gospel, because it is the power of God for the salvation of everyone who believes (Romans 1:16).

A two thousand-year-old letter still sends shock waves every time it is read.

Why? Because it leads the reader to "the power of God for salvation."

The apostle Paul had never been to Rome—the most important city of his day—but the message of his letter to the believers living there was crucial: how to find peace with God. H.A. Ironside sets the stage for Paul's "letter of life."

Walk With H.A. Ironside

"Romans gives us the fullest unfolding of the gospel that we have in the Word of God. It answers every objection of the most astute reasoner. It satisfies the need of every troubled conscience.

"In it we see how God can be just and yet justify the guilty sinner who comes to him in repentance, admitting his need and trusting his grace.

"The Greek philosopher Socrates exclaimed, 'It may be that the deity can forgive sins, but I don't see how!' The Holy Spirit shows here in Romans that God can forgive in righteousness because of the sacrificial work of his Son.

"This is the message which is revealed on the principle of faith to those who believe, whether Jews or Gentiles by birth, according to the words given to Habakkuk so long ago, 'The righteous will live by his faith.'"

Walk Closer to God

Socrates was asking the right question: "How can God forgive sins?" Paul supplies the right answer: "Only through his Son Jesus Christ."

Many have sought elsewhere for forgiveness of sins, purpose for living, fellowship with God. Romans points the way to the new life Christ has for all who will come.

Wouldn't you agree that's good news everyone needs to hear? Then don't be ashamed to proclaim what God was not ashamed to provide. ❍

JUNE 2

 Walk in the Word
Romans 1:18–32

Paul graphically depicts the unrighteousness of humanity, here highlighting the sin of Gentiles, who knew God only through creation.

God's Wrath Against Mankind

18The wrath of God is being revealed from heaven against all the godlessness and wickedness of men who suppress the truth by their wickedness, 19since what may be known about God is plain to them, because God has made it plain to them. 20For since the creation of the world God's invisible qualities — his eternal power and divine nature — have been clearly seen, being understood from what has been made, so that men are without excuse.

21For although they knew God, they neither glorified him as God nor gave thanks to him, but their thinking became futile and their foolish hearts were darkened. 22Although they claimed to be wise, they became fools 23and exchanged the glory of the immortal God for images made to look like mortal man and birds and animals and reptiles.

24Therefore God gave them over in the sinful desires of their hearts to sexual impurity for the degrading of their bodies with one another. 25They exchanged the truth of God for a lie, and worshiped and served created things rather than the Creator — who is forever praised. Amen.

26Because of this, God gave them over to shameful lusts. Even their women exchanged natural relations for unnatural ones. 27In the same way the men also abandoned natural relations with women and were inflamed with lust for one another. Men committed indecent acts with other men, and received in themselves the due penalty for their perversion.

28Furthermore, since they did not think it worthwhile to retain the knowledge of God, he gave them over to a depraved mind, to do what ought not to be done. 29They have become filled with every kind of wickedness, evil, greed and depravity. They are full of envy, murder, strife, deceit and malice. They are gossips, 30slanderers, God-haters, insolent, arrogant and boastful; they invent ways of doing evil; they disobey their parents; 31they are senseless, faithless, heartless, ruthless. 32Although they know God's righteous decree that those who do such things deserve death, they not only continue to do these very things but also approve of those who practice them.

Pictured in Nature, Proclaimed in Christ

God's invisible qualities—his eternal power and divine nature—have been clearly seen (Romans 1:20).

Elizabeth Barrett Browning was right:
Earth's crammed with heaven,
and every common bush aflame with God;
But only those who see take off their shoes;
The rest sit round it and pluck blackberries.
Hebrews puts it this way: "Anyone who comes to him must believe that he exists" (Hebrews 11:6).
A.W. Pink explains how that belief is sparked by seeing the power of the Creator who made the world.

Walk With A.W. Pink

"To say that God is visible in nature is true, yet it is a statement which needs qualifying.

"Nature reveals the existence of God, but it tells us little of his character. Nature demonstrates his natural qualities—his power, his wisdom, his unchanging character; but what does it say to us of his moral attributes—his justice, his holiness, his grace, his love? Nature, as such, knows no mercy or pity.

"If a blind saint unwittingly steps off a cliff, he meets with the same fate as if a murderer had stepped off. If I break nature's laws, no matter how sincere may be my subsequent repentance, there is no escaping the penalty.

"In this way we may say that nature conceals as well as reveals God."

Walk Closer to God

Creation shows God's grandeur and power; Jesus Christ shows his compassion. What is pictured in nature is proclaimed in Jesus Christ.

Sadly, what most people know of God, they choose to ignore. And though the choice is theirs, the consequences are not.

Consider carefully before you come to the foolish conclusion, "There is no God" (Psalm 14:1). For if you close your eyes to the telltale signs of his existence, you have no one but yourself to blame for the consequences.

JUNE 3

 Walk in the Word
Romans 2:1–16

*Paul outlines principles governing divine judgment against human sin;
these principles set the stage for the condemnation of Jews as well.*

God's Righteous Judgment

2 You, therefore, have no excuse, you who pass judgment on someone
else, for at whatever point you judge the other, you are condemning
yourself, because you who pass judgment do the same things. ²Now we
know that God's judgment against those who do such things is based on
truth. ³So when you, a mere man, pass judgment on them and yet do the
same things, do you think you will escape God's judgment? ⁴Or do you
show contempt for the riches of his kindness, tolerance and patience, not
realizing that God's kindness leads you toward repentance?

⁵But because of your stubbornness and your unrepentant heart, you are
storing up wrath against yourself for the day of God's wrath, when his
righteous judgment will be revealed. ⁶God "will give to each person according to what he has done."*a* ⁷To those who by persistence in doing
good seek glory, honor and immortality, he will give eternal life. ⁸But for
those who are self-seeking and who reject the truth and follow evil, there
will be wrath and anger. ⁹There will be trouble and distress for every human being who does evil: first for the Jew, then for the Gentile; ¹⁰but glory,
honor and peace for everyone who does good: first for the Jew, then for
the Gentile. ¹¹For God does not show favoritism.

¹²All who sin apart from the law will also perish apart from the law, and
all who sin under the law will be judged by the law. ¹³For it is not those
who hear the law who are righteous in God's sight, but it is those who obey
the law who will be declared righteous. ¹⁴(Indeed, when Gentiles, who do
not have the law, do by nature things required by the law, they are a law
for themselves, even though they do not have the law, ¹⁵since they show
that the requirements of the law are written on their hearts, their con-
sciences also bearing witness, and their thoughts now accusing, now even
defending them.) ¹⁶This will take place on the day when God will judge
men's secrets through Jesus Christ, as my gospel declares.

a6 Psalm 62:12; Prov. 24:12

Good News About the Law

For it is not those who hear the law who are righteous in God's sight, but it is those who obey the law who will be declared righteous (Romans 2:13).

High above the gorge, a tightrope walker balances precariously. Every muscle and nerve and thought is trained on just one objective: to stay on the thin strand of wire!

Few would volunteer for such a hazardous high-wire act. Yet many attempt something infinitely more dangerous. They try to find acceptance with God by keeping the law.

And, as John Wesley suggests, that's an exercise as unforgiving as a tightrope, for one mistake and the whole effort is futile.

Walk With John Wesley

"When people seek to establish their own righteousness, they do not consider what kind of obedience the law indispensably requires. It must be perfect and complete in every point or it does not answer the demands of the law.

"But which of you is able to perform such obedience? Who can fulfill every jot and tittle of the outward commandments of God, doing nothing which he forbids? Leaving nothing undone which he demands? Speaking no idle word?

"And how much less are you able to fulfill all the inward commandments of God—those which require that every mood and motion should be holiness unto the Lord!

"Are you able to love God with all your heart? To love all mankind as your own soul? To keep every affection, desire, and thought in obedience to his law?"

Walk Closer to God

Just as one crack in a mirror makes it a broken mirror, so one violation of God's law makes you a lawbreaker. But there is good news.

Though you cannot keep the law, the law can lead you to someone who can, and did, keep the law on your behalf. And he paid the penalty for the law you break.

That someone is the Savior—Christ the Lord. Is he your Savior?

JUNE 4

 Walk in the Word
Romans 2:17–29

Paul shines the light of God's judgment on self-righteousness and hypocrisy, revealing the necessity of inner renewal by the power of the Spirit.

The Jews and the Law

¹⁷Now you, if you call yourself a Jew; if you rely on the law and brag about your relationship to God; ¹⁸if you know his will and approve of what is superior because you are instructed by the law; ¹⁹if you are convinced that you are a guide for the blind, a light for those who are in the dark, ²⁰an instructor of the foolish, a teacher of infants, because you have in the law the embodiment of knowledge and truth— ²¹you, then, who teach others, do you not teach yourself? You who preach against stealing, do you steal? ²²You who say that people should not commit adultery, do you commit adultery? You who abhor idols, do you rob temples? ²³You who brag about the law, do you dishonor God by breaking the law? ²⁴As it is written: "God's name is blasphemed among the Gentiles because of you."[a]

²⁵Circumcision has value if you observe the law, but if you break the law, you have become as though you had not been circumcised. ²⁶If those who are not circumcised keep the law's requirements, will they not be regarded as though they were circumcised? ²⁷The one who is not circumcised physically and yet obeys the law will condemn you who, even though you have the[b] written code and circumcision, are a lawbreaker.

²⁸A man is not a Jew if he is only one outwardly, nor is circumcision merely outward and physical. ²⁹No, a man is a Jew if he is one inwardly; and circumcision is circumcision of the heart, by the Spirit, not by the written code. Such a man's praise is not from men, but from God.

[a]24 Isaiah 52:5; Ezek. 36:22   [b]27 Or *who, by means of a*

Worship
From The HEART

Examine your heart and make sure the sacrifice you offer is not blemished by self-deception. You come to God on the basis of your relationship with Jesus, not because of anything you have to offer. Praise God for providing a way of reconciliation through Jesus Christ.

Outward Ritual or Inward Relationship

A man is not a Jew if he is only one outwardly, . . . a man is a Jew if he is one inwardly (Romans 2:28–29).

What you act like on the outside. What you are on the inside. Are they the same? Or different?

The Jews of Paul's day had laws, customs and holidays that reminded them that they were a religious people, a God-centered society.

But they mistook knowing about God for knowing God—a mistake many duplicate today. Outwardly, they honored God with their lips. But inwardly, they dishonored him with their hearts.

W.H. Griffith Thomas offers this caution about confusing head knowledge with heart knowledge in your relationship with God.

Walk with W.H. Griffith Thomas

"Nothing is easier than self-righteousness and self-deception in religion.

"It is possible—without any real change of heart—to know a great deal of Christian truth, to be occupied with Christian work, to be associated with Christian people, to know with great familiarity Christian jargon, to live largely in a Christian atmosphere, yet all the while be without the new life that comes from the Spirit of God.

"The danger of such a position is far greater than that of willful and deliberate sin. Our Lord was constantly warning his hearers against such false assumptions."

Walk Closer to God

The Jews thought they were close to God. In reality, they were an eternity away.

Jesus warned, "Many will say to me on that day, 'Lord, Lord.' Then I will tell them plainly, 'I never knew you. Away from me.' " Hard words. Words that remind you that Christianity is more than facts and actions. It involves an inward transformation of heart.

You can fool your friends with the things you know . . . the words you use . . . the good works you do. But outward ritual can never replace the inward relationship God wants to have with you today—and every day! ◯

JOHN WESLEY

(1703–1791) PREACHER ON HORSEBACK AND FOUNDER OF METHODISM

A Heart Strangely Warmed

In 1662 the Industrial Revolution was in full swing, bringing sudden prosperity and, with it, low morality and religious indifference. Into this sin-filled scene John Wesley was born on June 17, 1703. Under his mother's influence, John quickly developed in spiritual and academic matters. At ten he began to learn Greek, Latin and theology; at twenty-one he graduated from Oxford and three years later received his master's degree.

Together with his brother Charles and George Whitefield, they formed the "Holy Club"—a group dedicated to prayer, Bible study and outreach. After a three-year stint in America, where John felt a growing sense of emptiness and a lack of confidence in his own salvation, he returned to England. On May 24, 1738, an event changed his life: "In the evening I went very unwillingly to a society at Aldersgate Street, where one was reading Luther's preface to the Epistle to the Romans. About a quarter before nine, while he was describing the change that God works in the heart through faith in Jesus Christ, I felt my heart strangely warmed. I felt I did trust in Christ, Christ alone, for my salvation; and an assurance was given me that he had taken away my sins."

After his conversion, Wesley took to the open air, preaching everywhere in England. He averaged 800 sermons a year—more than two a day—to crowds numbering as large as 20,000. Religious revival overtook England and the church was restored to life and activity.

The same Word of God that transformed John Wesley's life still changes lives, mends homes and restores morality. Today can be the beginning of a new revival in your life. But to obey God's Word you must know it. And to know it you must read it.

A LESSON FROM THE LIFE OF JOHN WESLEY

My unyielding obedience to God in his power can make a difference in my world.

JUNE 5

 Walk in the Word
Romans 3:1–20

After exposing the folly of possible arguments that would justify human unrighteousness, Paul concludes, with Old Testament support, that all humans are under the power of sin.

God's Faithfulness

3 What advantage, then, is there in being a Jew, or what value is there in circumcision? ²Much in every way! First of all, they have been entrusted with the very words of God.

³What if some did not have faith? Will their lack of faith nullify God's faithfulness? ⁴Not at all! Let God be true, and every man a liar. As it is written:

> "So that you may be proved right when you speak
> and prevail when you judge."ᵃ

⁵But if our unrighteousness brings out God's righteousness more clearly, what shall we say? That God is unjust in bringing his wrath on us? (I am using a human argument.) ⁶Certainly not! If that were so, how could God judge the world? ⁷Someone might argue, "If my falsehood enhances God's truthfulness and so increases his glory, why am I still condemned as a sinner?" ⁸Why not say—as we are being slanderously reported as saying and as some claim that we say—"Let us do evil that good may result"? Their condemnation is deserved.

No One Is Righteous

⁹What shall we conclude then? Are we any betterᵇ? Not at all! We have already made the charge that Jews and Gentiles alike are all under sin. ¹⁰As it is written:

> "There is no one righteous, not even one;
> ¹¹ there is no one who understands,
>   no one who seeks God.
> ¹²All have turned away,
>   they have together become worthless;
>   there is no one who does good,
>   not even one."ᶜ
> ¹³"Their throats are open graves;
>   their tongues practice deceit."ᵈ
>   "The poison of vipers is on their lips."ᵉ
> ¹⁴ "Their mouths are full of cursing and bitterness."ᶠ
> ¹⁵"Their feet are swift to shed blood;
> ¹⁶ ruin and misery mark their ways,
> ¹⁷and the way of peace they do not know."ᵍ
> ¹⁸ "There is no fear of God before their eyes."ʰ

473

JUNE 5

[19]Now we know that whatever the law says, it says to those who are under the law, so that every mouth may be silenced and the whole world held accountable to God. [20]Therefore no one will be declared righteous in his sight by observing the law; rather, through the law we become conscious of sin.

a4 Psalm 51:4   b9 Or *worse*   c12 Psalms 14:1-3; 53:1-3; Eccles. 7:20   d13 Psalm 5:9
e13 Psalm 140:3   f14 Psalm 10:7   g17 Isaiah 59:7,8   h18 Psalm 36:1

PSALM 119a

א Aleph

Blessed are they whose ways are blameless,
   who walk according to the law of the LORD.
[2]Blessed are they who keep his statutes
   and seek him with all their heart.
[3]They do nothing wrong;
   they walk in his ways.
[4]You have laid down precepts
   that are to be fully obeyed.
[5]Oh, that my ways were steadfast
   in obeying your decrees!
[6]Then I would not be put to shame
   when I consider all your commands.
[7]I will praise you with an upright heart
   as I learn your righteous laws.
[8]I will obey your decrees;
   do not utterly forsake me.

aThis psalm is an acrostic poem; the verses of each stanza begin with the same letter of the Hebrew alphabet.
